What people are saying about …

THE SACRED SEARCH

"Singles, pay attention. Gary knows marriage and is eager to help those of us desiring marriage get there with confidence and grace."

Lisa Anderson, Focus on the Family
director of young adults and host of
The Boundless Show, www.boundless.org

"It's what drives so many industries and even more individuals: it's the pursuit of the perfect spouse. But what if there's more—*much more*—to dating than finding 'the one'? In *The Sacred Search,* my friend Gary Thomas looks at the heart of a subject that many consider him an expert on—successful marriage. And with a biblical and bold approach, he shows readers that marriage isn't just about who we walk down the aisle with, but also about the very reasons behind that walk. Anyone who is dating, engaged, or hopes to be one day needs to read this book!"

Ed Young, senior pastor of Fellowship Church,
author of the *New York Times* best-seller *Sexperiment*

"Gary Thomas has logged a lot of miles working with young men and women as they navigate the often difficult path to marriage in the twenty-first century. *The Sacred Search* will help those who desire marriage to pursue it in a manner that deepens their faith, honors God, and blesses their future spouse."

Jim Daly, president of Focus on the Family

"Gary Thomas debunks the mythical search for a soul mate to help you choose a 'sole mate'—someone who will 'lay down their life' in faithful love. This biblically based book is for anyone who wants to be wise in their pursuit of a spouse."

Drs. Les and Leslie Parrott, authors of
Saving Your Marriage Before It Starts

"You may know *Sacred Marriage*. *The Sacred Search* will ask you why you want to be married. Filled with questions to make you think and teaching that will bring 'aha' moments, this book is a must-read for everyone considering marriage. I highly recommend it to you—I wish I'd had it when I was single!"

Linda Dillow, author of best-selling *Calm My Anxious Heart* and *What's It Like to Be Married to Me?*

"*The Sacred Search* is a powerfully honest portrayal of the biblical view of marriage. Gary Thomas dismantles contemporary philosophies on love, sexuality, and marital union by offering strong arguments for why they have not been successful. His comprehensive look at romantic relationships through psychological, emotional, physical, and spiritual perspectives gives the reader a framework for understanding the *why* of marriage in a world that is grossly fixated on the *who*. His appeal to a kingdom-first perspective gives both hope and healing for a generation in desperate need of a fresh and Christ-centered understanding of God's plan for marriage. This book is a must-read before anyone says 'I do.'"

Michelle Anthony, Family Ministry Architect for
David C Cook and author of *Spiritual Parenting*
and *Dreaming of More for the Next Generation*

"Our culture is obsessed with compatibility and chemistry. However, in relationship formation, character always trumps chemistry. Great marriages do not flow from compatibility; they flow from character. I appreciate Gary Thomas taking such a bold stand on marriage. *The Sacred Search* is a gut check for anyone considering, delaying, or even pursuing marriage. If marriage scares you, read this book and be encouraged. If you feel you are not ready for marriage, then please read and be prepared. If the critics tell you it ain't worth it, I beg you to read this book and learn how to honor marriage."

Ted Cunningham, author of *Young and in Love* and *Trophy Child*

"One of the primary hopes I have for my generation is that we will desire partnerships with purpose. In this book, Gary creates a compelling argument that shifts the believer's view of relationships, dating, and marriage to focus on something greater. His biblical, logical, and fatherly wise advice is the reason I will point my generation to his book for many of the commonly asked 'What about …' questions. And I will point the older generation to him as a guide to mentoring my peers. I'm thankful Gary has created this resource. Guess I can quit my job now!"

Joy Eggerichs, director of Love and Respect (Now)

"Something is broken. Marriages are falling apart all around us, and I believe Gary Thomas has just gone straight to the root. We build our entire lives on this earth around this one decision (who to marry): where we live, how we live. Even future humans hang in the balance. Gary just built a map to help you see through the emotion and infatuation to God's heart for dating and marriage."

Jennie Allen, author of *Anything*

"In *The Sacred Search,* Gary Thomas clearly, relevantly, and scripturally debunks common myths that stunt singles. He helps us see the fallacy of searching for our 'soul mate' and waiting around for 'the one.' This book will help singles make wiser choices about who we marry because it explores why we marry."

Lindsey Nobles, blogger, www.lindseynobles.com

"'Why should I get married?' could be the most important question millennials are asking. Gary Thomas helps this generation navigate the 'why' in a Christ-honoring way. A long-awaited tool for how singles can navigate the difficult waters of dating and how to make finding a mate a holy pursuit."

Esther Fleece, millennial expert (former assistant to the president for millennial relations at Focus on the Family)

"Gary Thomas's *The Sacred Search* is a very powerful look at what it means to put God first in all of life, especially dating and relationships. Practical, wise, and thoroughly Biblical, this is a perfect resource for anyone seeking direction in finding a lifelong relationship in a way that honors God. I got a lot out of it personally and pass it on with great enthusiasm to those in the sacred search."

Jud Wilhite, senior pastor of Central Christian Church, author of *The God of Yes*

GARY THOMAS

THE

SACRED

SEARCH

WHAT IF IT'S NOT ABOUT WHO YOU MARRY, BUT WHY?

DAVID C COOK

transforming lives together

THE SACRED SEARCH
Published by David C Cook
4050 Lee Vance Drive
Colorado Springs, CO 80918 U.S.A.

Integrity Music Limited, a Division of David C Cook
Brighton, East Sussex BN1 2RE, England

The graphic circle C logo is a registered trademark of David C Cook.

The website addresses recommended throughout this book are offered as a resource to you. These websites are not intended in any way to be or imply an endorsement on the part of David C Cook, nor do we vouch for their content.

Some names have been changed to protect privacy. Permission has been obtained for usage of all other personal accounts.

All Scripture quotations, unless otherwise noted, are taken from the Holy Bible, New International Version®, NIV®. Copyright © 1973, 1984 by Biblica, Inc.™ Used by permission of Zondervan. All rights reserved worldwide. www.zondervan. com. Scripture quotations marked NIV 2011 are taken from the Holy Bible, New International Version®, NIV®. Copyright © 1973, 2011 by Biblica, Inc.™ Used by permission of Zondervan. All rights reserved worldwide. www.zondervan.com; NKJV are taken from the New King James Version®. Copyright © 1982 by Thomas Nelson, Inc. Used by permission. All rights reserved; ESV are taken from The Holy Bible, English Standard Version® (ESV®), copyright © 2001 by Crossway, a publishing ministry of Good News Publishers. Used by permission. All rights reserved; NASB are taken from the New American Standard Bible®, Copyright © 1960, 1995 by The Lockman Foundation. Used by permission. (www.Lockman. org.) The author has added italics to Scripture quotations for emphasis.

Library of Congress Control Number 2012951904
ISBN 978-1-4347-0489-4
eISBN 978-1-4347-0554-9

© 2013 Gary Thomas
Published in associations with Yates & Yates, www.yates2.com.

The Team: Alex Field, Karen Lee-Thorp, Amy Konyndyk,
Nick Lee, Caitlyn Carlson, Karen Athen
Cover Design: JWH Garphic Arts, James Hall

Printed in the United States of America
First Edition 2013

17 18 19 20 21 22 23 24 25 26

110519

To two very special people: my oldest brother, Jerry Thomas, who has been a rock in our family and a great encouragement and inspiration to me for my entire life, and to his delightful daughter (and my goddaughter), Lindsey Thomas, that she will embrace the godly example her parents have set for her and enjoy the riches of a truly sacred marriage.

ACKNOWLEDGMENTS

I'd like to thank those who read previous versions of this book and offered many helpful comments: Lisa Thomas, Darrell and Allison Vesterfelt, Steve and Rebecca Wilke, Mary Kay Smith, John Card, Steve and Candice Watters, Lindsey Thomas, and Jay Fields. A special thanks is also due to Dr. Ed Young and our home church, Second Baptist in Houston, Texas, for the support base they provide.

I am also very grateful to my agent, Curtis Yates of Yates and Yates, for his friendship and partnership for so many years; and to the David C Cook team: especially Alex Field, Dan Rich, Don Pape, Mike Salisbury, Ginia Croker, Karen Lee-Thorp, Caitlyn Carlson, Mike Worley, Michael Covington, Ingrid Beck, and the many other fine individuals who have worked to make this book a success. It's an honor to be part of your team.

CONTENTS

I

A TALE OF TWO TEARS

The faithful pastor's face grew taut as he told me, "Let me be honest with you. My marriage has constituted the biggest cross of my life."

The tears that slipped out of his eyes and rolled down his cheeks provided a sobering picture of the weight this man carries with him every day of his life. Instead of launching him into newer and bigger opportunities, instead of providing encouragement and sustenance and hope, his marriage is acting like dead weight. God continues to use him, but he walks his journey with a rock in his shoe that hurts him every step of the way.

A thirtysomething woman looked into my eyes and let tears of another sort flow freely as she spoke of her husband's care for her. She's had some health-related issues to contend with, and life has not been easy, but her husband has been another kind of rock, a source of tremendous encouragement and acceptance: "Next to Jesus, my husband has been the greatest joy in my life. I can't even imagine where I'd be without him or how I would have faced all that I have without him by my side."

Both of these scenarios are true. I'm sorry that they may reinforce gender stereotypes—the male leader and the woman needing support. Because they are based in fact I can't, with integrity, change them. Look past that for a moment to see the real-life frustration and joy, respectively, that each person feels. One person is crying tears of pain, working as hard as he can to keep his marriage together, but his relationship is compared to a cross. It saps his strength, but he perseveres, because he knows it's the right thing to do.

The other person is also crying, but not because she is struggling through a difficult relationship. She weeps because she is grateful for a man who loves her so well, so wonderfully, that she can't imagine life without him.

Tears of pain and tears of joy.

A marriage compared to bearing the cross.

A union compared to a foretaste of heaven.

Ten years after you're married, what kind of tears will you be crying? Will they be the stinging tears of pain or warm tears generated by joy? The reality is, every marriage has plenty of both kinds of tears, but it's also true that some marriages are marked primarily by pain while others are marked primarily by joy. No marriage is easy, but some marriages build each partner up, while others tear each partner down. Every marriage takes time and effort, but some marriages sap the spouses' strength, while others generate joy and enthusiasm and intimacy.

I'm writing this book because I want you to cry tears of joy on your tenth anniversary. I want you to be able to say, with all sincerity,

"Next to becoming a Christian, marrying _____ is the best decision I've ever made."

But here's the thing that might shock you: the answer to this
question may well be driven more by why you get married than by
who you marry. It's not that the "who" doesn't matter (in fact, it matters very much); it's just that asking and settling the "why" question
first will set you up to make a wise choice about the "who." Why
do you want to get married? That's what you need to ask before you
decide *who* to marry.

It's a particularly important question because if you make one
bad financial investment, you can always start over, but biblical marriage is a one-shot deal. Many Christians believe there are a couple
of biblically "accepted" causes for divorce, but these are limited and
severe. In the vast majority of cases, should you become disappointed
in your choice, your obligation as a believer will be to work it out
instead of walking out and starting over. This fact alone makes it
doubly worth the time, effort, and even the heartache of a breakup
for believers to make sure they're making a wise decision before they
enter into marriage. Once you get married, every evening, every
weekend, every holiday, every morning will be marked, for good or
for ill, by that relationship.

The person you marry is the last person you'll see every night
before you go to sleep. Their face is the first one you will see when
you wake up in the morning. Their words will encourage or discour-
age you, their humor will make you laugh in amusement or cry in
shame. Their body will pleasure you or threaten you. Their hands
will hold you or hurt you. Their presence will be a healing balm or a
reminder of all that could have been.

Many years ago, when speaking at an event in California, I slipped out of a hotel ballroom in order to pick up an extra shirt at an outside mall (poor packing). Surrounded by beautiful people in a beautiful setting, I longed more than I can describe to see my wife walking toward me. I had a *fantasy* about my wife, but there was nothing sexual about it. I just wanted to see her walking out of that mass of people and smiling in my direction, to know she would spend the rest of the weekend with me. It was an impossible fantasy—Lisa was a thousand miles away, just north of Seattle, caring for our children, but there wasn't a sight in the world that would have given me more joy that day than to see Lisa—my wife—walking toward me.

I want you to have moments like that—where, even when you're apart, you wish you could be together. I don't want you to be like so many couples I talk to whose fantasy is watching their spouses walk *away.*

It changes you as a person when a woman who calls you her pastor is crying on the phone because she's worried that your work with her husband will cause him to *stay.* She's exhausted by her marriage, disappointed to the extreme, ready for it to be over with—but she wants to honor God, so she and her husband meet with you. She then listens to you talk and thinks God might actually use you to convince her husband to fully repent and change his ways, and that's what causes her to break down. She and her husband had a good nine months of dating, but there hasn't been a good nine-month stretch in their entire ten-year marriage, and his divorcing her would feel like liberation.

I don't want that for you. I don't want you ever to be at a point where you think your happiness as a spouse depends upon my failure as a pastor to convince your spouse to stay. But, friends, that's real life for a lot of couples. They rushed the process or made the decision for poor reasons and now are fighting the consequences every day of their lives.

LIFE-GIVING LOVE

So let's briefly introduce the "why" of marriage to set you up to make a wise choice about the "who." A home established on Matthew 6:33—"Seek first the kingdom of God and His righteousness, and all these things shall be added to you" (NKJV)—is a glorious thing. While this verse contains a command, it's also an exciting promise of a rich and meaningful life. When husband and wife are committed in Christ, growing together in the Lord, supporting each other in their spiritual walks, raising children in the fear of the Lord, loving each other out of reverence for God, joy abounds and miracles happen. Selfish people become servants. Self-centered children grow up to become workers in God's kingdom. Strangers become intimate friends. Daily life is filled with the drama of kingdom building. There are plenty of mistakes, lots of repenting, times of frustration, sickness, and even doubts. But in the end, God's presence prevails, people are transformed, kingdom work is accomplished, and trials are overcome. If two people join themselves around this mission—if they make their marital choice based on the best person with whom they can accomplish this mission—they are far more likely to have a fulfilling and soul-building marriage.

On the other hand, I've witnessed how miserable people can make each other when they live for themselves. Though their initial sexual attraction might have been off the charts, it is usually only a matter of months until they are saying and doing awful, awful things to each other, so awful that they will call a pastor on the phone, someone they don't even know, because they are so desperate to find another way to live. There was a time when they couldn't live without each other; every second, they had to be together. They couldn't keep their hands off each other. Now they can't bear to live together. When they're in the same room, or in the same car, or on the same telephone call, they can't stop fighting.

It's made me realize that the old cliché is all too true: a good marriage is the closest two people will ever come to heaven this side of eternity; a bad marriage is the closest two people in an affluent society will ever come to hell.

Such problems usually erupt from trying to build a life together without purpose, without mission, without something that not only establishes a connection but keeps you caring about each other for the next fifty to sixty years.

Can I be honest with you? There isn't a person alive who can keep you enthralled for the next five or six decades. If they're really funny, really attractive, and you're really infatuated, you can be enthralled for a few years, but selfish people—even wealthy selfish people, or beautiful selfish people, or famous selfish people—eventually get bored with each other, and the very relationship that once gave them security and life feels like prison and death. No matter how intensely you feel in love now, the same thing will happen to you if you get married without a shared mission.

I want you to have a spiritually enriching marriage, a marriage that spawns life, vibrancy, intimacy, a lifetime of memories with your best friend, and the overwhelming joy of creating a family together. Family life is such a good life, and intimate marriage is such an amazing gift. The friendship that results from facing all seasons of life together, praying together, raising kids together, serving the Lord together, having fun, having sex, suffering heartaches and heartbreaks, overcoming setbacks and learning to deal with disappointments, growing together through all of them, creates a bond that no initial sexual attraction or romantic infatuation could ever hope to match.

The reward for making a wise marital choice is so tremendous that I don't want you to miss it. The consequences of making a foolish choice can be so painful and lasting that I don't want you to have to endure them.

I cannot overstate how crucial it is to be cautious and discerning in making such an important decision. You don't want to miss out, do you? This is not a time for romanticized foolishness. If you remain rooted in Christ, fully engage your mind, and draw on all your resources—God's guidance, Scripture, your family, your church, your sensible friends—and approach this decision with all intention, purpose, and wisdom, you are far more likely to enter a rich, satisfying, and soul-building marriage.

Ask yourself: "Ten years from now, what kind of tears do I want to be crying? Tears of joy, or tears of pain? Do I want to be in a marriage that lifts me up, or one that drags me down? A union marked by a shared partnership, or one where we're hiding from and hurting each other on a regular basis?"

Stick with me, and I'll do everything I can to help you cry tears of joy.

STUDY QUESTIONS

1. Describe a marriage you respect: what is it about the couple that makes you admire their relationship?

2. Ten years after you're married, how do you hope someone will describe your marriage relationship? Write out the "ideal" description of the relationship you hope to have.

3. Describe some of the marriages you've seen that you definitely do not want to model your own marriage on. What attributes of those relationships do you hope to avoid?

4. Have you ever asked yourself the question, "Why do I want to get married?" Why do you want to get married?

5. How do you think getting married with the intention of "seeking first the kingdom of God" will change the way you pursue someone to marry, as well as the type of person you might consider?

2

THE GREAT EXCEPTION

Can you help me out here? There must be a version of the Bible out there I haven't read yet, one that has a mysterious exception clause.

I thought I had the bases covered in my research. I've checked out the King James, the English Standard Version, the New King James, the New International Version (both the 1984 and the 2011 editions), the Message, the New Living Translation, the New American Standard, and many others. None of them—not one—contains the exception clause I'm looking for, so if you find it, will you please email me and let me know which version has it? Because apparently it's the version many singles read.

The exception clause I'm referring to is found in Matthew 6:33. Here's how it reads in the New King James Version: "Seek first the kingdom of God and His righteousness, and all these things shall be added to you."

The mysterious version I'm looking for, the one I see so many people following and memorizing, goes something like this: "Seek first the kingdom of God and His righteousness, *except when you're choosing someone to marry. In that case, you should follow your emotions, insist on a thrilling romantic attraction and overall relational compatibility that makes the relationship fun*, and then all these things will be added unto you."

Let me ask you: do you trust Jesus? Do you believe that He truly has your best interests at heart, that He would never mislead you—that if you follow His advice, you're setting yourself up for the best, most meaningful, and most fulfilling life imaginable? Can you count on Him knowing what He's talking about? Do you think it's possible that the second most important decision you'll ever make—who you marry—should be based on Jesus's fundamental agenda for our lives: seeking first God's kingdom and righteousness? Do you believe every significant decision we make should be run through this grid? If our choice of marital partner is an exception, what *wouldn't* qualify as an exception? If Jesus's words aren't relevant for such a crucial decision, why would they have any importance in any lesser decision?

I want to make a promise to you: if you will seek first God's kingdom and His righteousness and let that agenda drive your decision regarding whom you choose to marry and refuse to compromise on that, you will set yourself up for a much more fulfilling, spiritually enriching, and overall more satisfying marriage. *The degree to which you compromise on this verse is the degree to which you put your future satisfaction in jeopardy and open wide the door to great frustration and even regret.*

WHY WE MARRY

If you're under thirty years old, your generation is the first generation in about a hundred years not to assume that you need to call the phone company when you move into a new apartment or house. In my day, that was one of the first things we did—at college, and then afterward. We "hooked up the phones" so that people could get in touch with us.

Cell phones have demolished that assumption. Most people under thirty don't even have what used to be referred to as "land lines." If someone wants to reach you, they have your cell phone; why pay for a line inside your house?

And yet every month, millions of older people who own cell phones *still* pay thirty to forty dollars to maintain a home phone line, just because they always have.

You can laugh at your parents for not getting how the world has moved on, but there are a few things singles are susceptible to, things you take for granted, that just aren't true either. Even so, you keep on doing them, because everyone you know blindly accepts certain assumptions—such as the belief that you should seek romantic excitement and sexual chemistry above everything else when it comes to choosing someone to marry.

Our culture is still stuck on viewing marriage through the lens of happiness first and foremost—defining happiness by romantic intensity and sexual chemistry. Since the 1960s, sociologists have found a steady progression of young American men and women who demand more and more of love—yet we're getting less and less out of our marriages. In 1967, a study of college-age women found that 76 percent of women said they would marry someone if the man had every trait they were looking for, even if they didn't feel "romantic love" toward them. In more recent research, 91 percent of women said "absolutely not."[1] That's a huge shift. People have been pursuing such pairings for several generations now, and I'm asking you to be an astute and honest observer: how's that working out for us?

For starters: how many marriages do you see that are truly happy? I'm not talking about marriages that are less than three years old. Tell me—how many people do you know who have been married ten years or longer whose marriage you envy or even admire?

Notice the trend: most people marry on the basis of perceived happiness, but few remain very happy for very long. And yet, every year, hundreds of thousands of couples think they can be different, so they base their decision *on the same premise*: we "feel" something special, we seem to be happy together, we're generally compatible, so let's get married.

How many failed marriages will it take for us to see that this approach just isn't working? Make this personal: why do you think it will be any different for you than it has been for the millions of other couples who have already tried this approach?

Are you willing to even consider that the Hollywood version of "falling in love" might just possibly be leading people astray? That, as powerful as romance is, it might not be the best reason to get married?

Here's just one quick example of how sexual chemistry, apart from any other consideration, can lead us astray. Psychologically, women are *more* likely to experience romantic love with dominant men, even though dominant men typically demonstrate *less* ability to express the kind of companionship, relational skills, and emotional attachment that women ultimately desire in a lifelong mate. In other words, women, if you simply follow your feelings, you are more likely to fall in love with a guy who will thrill you for twelve to eighteen months as a boyfriend and then frustrate you for five to six decades as a husband.

Guys, on the other hand, are more inclined to experience romantic love with women they are attracted to physically, yet physical appearance is the thing most likely to change in a person's life. Marriage isn't about being young together; it's about growing old together—and bodies change as we get older. If you don't marry with that in mind, you're going to make a major mistake—perhaps the biggest mistake of your life.

What draws most of us *into* marriage is rarely the ingredient that serves long-term happiness in marriage. Understanding this alone will help you make a wiser choice.

MAYBE BEING IN LOVE ISN'T ENOUGH

I had a sobering conversation with a woman my age. She's been divorced twice. She was getting serious with another guy, but things had gotten rocky and hurtful. It was so bad, her boyfriend made her cry a couple of times a week. He could be forceful, say mean things, and though he wasn't physically violent, he could scare her. There were, of course, several positive aspects about the relationship. He could be thoughtful, supportive, occasionally even poetic, but the negative things were, interestingly enough, the very same issues that had led to the breakup of her first two marriages, so you might think they'd be red flags for her. Why would she want to enter into another relationship that would make her miserable? To make matters worse, she wasn't sure she could trust him—in fact, she'd overheard him telling another woman on the phone that he still loved her. On its own, this seemed quite a devastating analysis, but here's the thing: she was still in the relationship.

I asked what seemed like some obvious questions: "Why are you still with him? What's in this for you? Why do you put up with this?"

Her response was immediate: "Because I'm in love with him. I genuinely and deeply love him."

I paused to set my tone on "as gentle as possible." This was a minefield, but I was afraid that if I didn't address the situation, this woman could make yet another serious mistake after already experiencing two blown marriages.

"Were you in love with your first husband?" I asked.

"Definitely. I was devastated when he cheated on me and then left me."

"And what about your second husband?"

"Yes. It was different, I think, because he fed some ego needs, but of course, I was in love with him."

"And yet both marriages failed."

"That's right."

I took a deep breath and tried be as gentle as I could be when I said, "Maybe feeling like you're in love with someone isn't enough of a reason for you to get married. Maybe you need to set the bar higher, find something more."

You won't hear a character's friend say this in a romantic comedy. Taylor Swift won't sing this, Eminem won't rap it, and Suzanne Collins won't write it, but it's true: *just because you're "in love" with someone doesn't mean you should seriously consider marrying them.* The next chapter will explain why I believe this is true, but for now I'm just throwing it out there and asking you to at least consider that romantic attraction, as wonderful and as emotionally intoxicating as it can be, can actually lead you astray as much as it can help you. I'm not talking it down; "connecting" with someone on that level is a wonderful thing. Enjoy it, revel in it, even write a song about it if you want, but *don't bet your life on it.*

I've seen infatuation lead far more people astray than into satisfying marriages. I've seen people fail to pursue a relationship, even though they respected, admired, and loved another person, because there didn't seem to be that over-the-top, make-my-knees-weak sexual chemistry. And I've watched people rush into a relationship that any objective observer could see had some serious problems on the horizon, but the feelings were *so intense*, it all felt *so right*, that two people were willing to bet their lives and their future kids' happiness on it.

I believe both Scripture and science testify that making a lifetime decision about who to marry primarily on the basis of romantic attraction is a very foolish thing to do.

STUDY QUESTIONS

1. If you personally know anyone who has gotten married recently, discuss why you think they got married. Were their decisions based on good reasons? What can you learn from watching others?

2. Do you agree with Gary that Matthew 6:33 should drive your pursuit of a marriage partner? Why or why not?

3. What would make you consider someone as a potential marriage partner? What would definitely disqualify a person in your mind?

4. What was your reaction to Gary's statement, "Just because you're 'in love' with someone doesn't mean you should seriously consider marrying them"?

5. How can you and your friends question your assumptions about why you should or shouldn't be interested in someone as "marriage material"? What assumptions do you need to question? What will it take to do that?

3

VULNERABLE AND STUPID

The way God made our brains, infatuation resembles an hourglass. The moment you become smitten by someone—the second you find yourself deeply "in love"—is the moment that hourglass gets turned over.

There is enough sand in that hourglass, on average, to last you about twelve to eighteen months. On occasion, the sand may trickle down a bit beyond that, up to about two years, but never by much and not with the same intensity. The average life span of an infatuation is almost always less than two years. Yeah, sexual chemistry and romantic attraction can remain. Certainly, during times of trauma or intimate connection, those romantic feelings will be revived, but they cease to be the main glue that holds a relationship together on a day-to-day basis. Feelings become "warm and dependable" more than "hot and excitable." God simply did not design our brains to sustain a lifelong infatuation (for some very good reasons).

How do you know if you're in an infatuation? Here are the neurological markers according to Dr. Helen Fisher, a preeminent biological anthropologist who has written on the topic:

- The lover focuses on the beloved's better traits and overlooks or minimizes flaws.
- Infatuated people exhibit extreme energy, hyperactivity, sleeplessness, impulsivity, euphoria, and mood swings.
- One or both of the partners develops a goal-oriented fixation on winning the beloved.
- Relational passion is heightened, not weakened, by adversity; the more the relationship is attacked, the more the passion grows.
- The lovers become emotionally dependent on the relationship.
- Partners reorder their daily priorities to remain in contact as much as humanly possible, and they even experience separation anxiety when apart.
- Empathy is so powerful that many report they would "die for their beloved."
- An infatuated person thinks about their lover to an obsessive degree.
- Sexual desire is intense, and the relationship becomes marked by extreme possessiveness.[1]

The way many researchers describe this brain state overall is an "idealization" of the one you love. You focus on strengths (many of which might be imaginary) and are blind to weaknesses (many of which are readily apparent to outside observers). You "idealize" this person to make them the kind of person you *want* them to be. It should be clear that in this state you're in no position to make an objective choice if you rely only on your feelings.

Here's what you're dealing with: "Romantic love is involuntary, difficult to control, and impermanent."[2] That's the *psychological* view, but let me say that as Christians, though the initial onslaught of feelings is involuntary, what we do with those feelings, how we control our thoughts, and the level of our obsessiveness is our responsibility. We may not be able to choose the initial onslaught, but we *can* choose how we manage it. We can feed it, starve it, indulge it, or test it.

We are not "evolved mammals" who must play out our biological destiny. We are image bearers of the Creator God, who has redeemed us and given us His Holy Spirit to empower us, correct us, and guide us.

We need to be wise about our human condition but place our hope in our spiritual redemption. It helps Christians to know that romantic love can spring on us unintended and that there is no age limit. You might be single in your twenties or married in your fifties; infatuation will take you through roughly the same emotions and process. Recognizing this, as well as infatuation's impermanence, helps us to be forewarned, so that when it happens we're not caught unprepared. It's a fact of life, but it's going to pass (at least in its current form). We all have to learn to deal with it and become good stewards of our emotional and relational health.

INFATUATED WITH INFATUATION

We live in a culture that is infatuated with infatuation, for some understandable reasons. Psychologists liken infatuation to an addiction; indeed, it affects the same regions of our brains as cocaine or gambling. Just as some people are more prone to alcoholism than others, however, some people are more genetically predisposed to "fall in love" more often and more intensely. This is an important point to keep in mind if the one you've given your heart to doesn't seem as "desperately" in love as you do. Infatuation doesn't affect everyone in the same way.

Neurologically, a person's sense of security, self-esteem, spiritual maturity, and personality all affect *how* they fall in love, *what* that experience feels like, and the *intensity* with which they feel those emotions. For example, an insecure person with low self-esteem is likely to be clingy and more obsessive about the relationship than someone who is relatively secure with a high self-esteem. A woman from a broken home who has a high fear of abandonment often wants to rush things to "lock in" the relationship, pushing for an early engagement. She's more concerned about avoiding another relational loss than she is about finding the best possible match. Two relatively secure individuals can respect and love each other without experiencing obsessive thinking, euphoric mood swings, or desperate clinginess. The absence of these markers doesn't mean they are less in love than other couples; it might just mean they are more grounded as individuals.

While the experience of infatuation is not exactly the same for any two individuals, when it comes, it is thrilling, powerful, promising, and even transcendent. I don't want to diminish the mystery and poetry of a truly delicious romantic attachment and "soul connection," but in reality you're living through a fairly predictable and observable neurochemical reaction. And here's something you need to know: the state of infatuation actually impedes your ability to objectively discern your partner's faults and weaknesses. Dr. Thomas Lewis put it this way: "Love may not be literally blind, but it does seem to be literally incapable of reason and the levels of appropriate negativity necessary for realism."[3]

One summer I spoke at a church in Pennsylvania, and a young woman came up to me afterward. She and her boyfriend were talking about marriage. She asked my advice, and we discussed her boyfriend's strengths. I then asked her about his weaknesses. She blushed a bit and answered, "You know, that's what's so amazing. I don't think he has any."

"Really?"

"I know. I can't believe it either. I guess I just got lucky."

I reminded her of James 3:2, "We *all* stumble in many ways," and said to her, "I'm going to trust the truth of Scripture—that we *all* stumble, including your boyfriend—more than I'll trust your perception. Since you asked for it, my advice is this: don't marry this guy until you can tell me how he stumbles, because I guarantee you—even more than that, *God's Word guarantees you*—that he does stumble, and you might as well know what you're signing up for before you marry him."

Here's the danger of letting these powerful feelings dictate whether you begin, stay in, or end a relationship: when the relationship hits a rough spot (as it inevitably will), most people who have overwhelming feelings will ignore the issues raised by the conflict and try to make the relationship work *because* they have strong feelings. Wisdom says we should try to make a relationship work not because we have strong feelings *but because it's a good match*. Far too often, we are more motivated to preserve the relationship if the feelings are there than if the match makes sense. In other words, most of us are motivated more by feelings than by wisdom.

A PREDICTABLE PATTERN

You "fall in love," and suddenly you have increased energy; your attention is focused, almost obsessive; you become possessive and then practically live to make this person your own. It's amazing to me how virtually every other tie in life is considered inferior and less important than this newfound emotion.

A woman once asked me to pray for her because she felt like she might "have" to leave the hometown she had lived in for over twenty-five years—a town where she was gainfully employed, where she had been a church member her entire life, where all her friends and family—not to mention her entire base of support—were.

"Why would you want to leave all this?" I asked.

"I think God may be leading me to," she replied.

It turned out that the motivation was actually a guy, not a God, and one who lived fifteen hundred miles away.

"He must be some guy," I said, "if you're willing to give up everything to follow him. Where did you meet him, if he lives so far away?"

There was a slight pause. "Well …"

"Online?" I suggested.

"Yes."

"So you haven't actually met him in person."

"No. But we've talked on the phone almost every day for weeks."

Let me state up front that I'm not a critic of some online dating websites. There are far worse ways to meet someone, and in fact, if it's a good site, it can be a valuable tool. No one need be embarrassed about meeting someone through a site like that. Marriage is a good thing, and being intentional about your pursuit of it is commendable, not shameful. Using modern technology to help you is something the church should applaud. But to talk about leaving your entire life behind for someone you've never even met face-to-face boggles my mind—yet that's how powerful infatuation can be. It can lead us to talk crazy and, even worse, act crazy.

In fact, studies suggest that romantic attachment is more powerful than the sex drive. Neurologically speaking, *it's easier to say no to physical sexual passion than it is to regulate the rush of emotional infatuation.* And men, don't think it's only women who read romance novels who are susceptible to this. Because men are attracted to physical appearance more than women are, most psychologists believe that more men than women experience "love at first sight."

If you've found yourself in the throes of an infatuation and acted foolishly, welcome to the club. It's not easy to learn how to manage these emotions, and you are far from the first person to say or do stupid things accordingly. But for now you need to understand that as soon as you become infatuated, you are vulnerable and stupid. I say this with all compassion. Don't trust yourself. Recognize what's going on, and set some safeguards (we'll talk about these later).

Since, according to Dr. Helen Fisher, "romantic love is tenacious and ... difficult to control," [4] you can expect that once you fall in love, it's hard to fall out of love until the neurochemical reaction fades. Your brain is focused on two tasks during infatuation: *getting* that person and *keeping* him or her. Your brain doesn't have anything left over to evaluate whether someone is *worth* getting or *worth* keeping. The person you're obsessed with can do some awful, awful things, but infatuation is not easily discarded. It'll hang in there and won't let go, despite all evidence that this isn't a person you should be with.

If you enter this battle without the guidance of friends, family members, and pastoral support, you're likely to ignore obvious cues and even defend indefensible behavior. You *can't* be fully objective when infatuation takes root, so it's foolish not to listen to others who aren't in the "crazy state" that you are.

A quick word to the older readers here, perhaps those who have a previous marriage in their past. Too many middle-aged people say, "I'm older, I've been married, I know what I want, so it's okay to cut corners here. We don't need to take the time to get to know each other." That's a very foolish mind-set. No matter how old you are, when infatuation gets hold of your brain, you're just as blind as an eighteen-year-old experiencing his or her first crush.

VULNERABLE

Not only are you stupid when you're infatuated, but you also become extremely vulnerable. I'm speaking as a pastor who has witnessed the tremendous pain that romanticism has led so many people into. Psychologically, "hearts broken from love lost rate among the most stressful life events a person can experience, exceeded in psychological pain only by horrific events such as a child dying."[5] If you dive in and let yourself go emotionally, without even knowing whether the person you are falling for is worthy of your trust, and that person then cheats on you or rejects you, the fact that they are of low character won't remove your pain. You'll feel tremendous loss.

It's not the same for everyone, of course, but some people have been known to die from a heart attack or stroke following depression caused by a romantic breakup. Neurologically, the pain of social rejection triggers some of the same systems that physical pain does in the brain. Your hurt is real, even though it's emotional.

Why do that to yourself?

This makes it equally dangerous to play with someone else's emotions. One psychologist talked about the horrific price some women pay when they emotionally entangle themselves with a man whom they later spurn. Some men react with rage (which is why you don't want to commit to a man until you know he can handle anger): "In our recent studies, we found that an alarming number of men who are unceremoniously dumped begin to have homicidal fantasies.... The loss of love is enough to make a man homicidal."[6]

Women, take note: "Roughly half of the women who are murdered in America every year are killed by the ones who presumably love them—their husbands, boyfriends, ex-husbands, or ex-boyfriends—in circumstances that are remarkably similar."[7] The murders are initiated by romantic love that was spurned or died.

Falling in love can be a very dangerous game. Be careful who you play it with.

And, men, it's just as dangerous to spurn a woman. Some years ago, a Houston woman became so angry when she found her husband with his mistress at a hotel that she got into her Mercedes-Benz and ran over him with her car. Still not satisfied, she circled the parking lot and ran over him *again*. Even that wasn't enough—she backed up and hit him yet a third time, pinning him under the car, while her daughter, who witnessed all this, cried out, "You killed my dad!" The spurned woman didn't stop until her car was literally on top of her husband.

Particularly heart wrenching is that, with the car's tire on top of her husband's body, the woman got out and apologized to him, telling him that she still loved him.[8]

Emotions are powerful things; don't play around with them. And make sure you are with someone who has power over his or her emotions. If I'm going to make myself extremely vulnerable with someone, I want that person to be ruled by the Holy Spirit, who can check those negative thoughts and actions, rather than, in biblical language, someone who is ruled by "the flesh."

WISDOM WAITS

All of this, I hope, is an argument for not getting married too hastily. Wisdom waits. Wisdom is patient. Blurting out or acting on your feelings in the bloom of their creation is a tempting but foolish thing to do: "Do you see a man who is hasty in his words? There is more hope for a fool than for him" (Prov. 29:20 ESV).

One young woman told my friend Virginia Friesen how she had found "the man of her dreams." She and her boyfriend had been together just three months but were already talking about marriage and even discussing setting a date for the wedding that would allow just enough time to plan the ceremony. The young woman told Virginia that her boyfriend was "everything she had ever hoped for, and so much different from the last man she dated." Virginia's response was classic and wise, and one I hope you'll consider: "At the three-month mark, my former boyfriend was also everything I had ever wanted. But by month six, the relationship fell apart."[9]

Dr. Fisher found huge discrepancies between the brain scans of couples who had been in love just about eight months and the scans of those who had been in love about twenty-eight months. Those together just over two years had a far more realistic view of their partner and their relationship than those who were still in the rush of infatuation.[10]

How many of your friends have told you, after being let down by someone they truly loved, "He's not the person I thought he was"? That's because he *wasn't*. That's a true observation! They were relating to an idealized (fictional) version of a man—or woman—not that person's authentic self.

Most couples won't wait two years, and since our brains vary, I'm not one to create an artificial barrier. I'm more concerned that you have progressed to the point where you have a reasonably accurate view of someone than that you've made it to a certain point on the calendar. Given all that we've looked at, however, I think wisdom says you're being a bit foolish if you get engaged in less than a year. If you get married sooner than that, at the very least you should do so with the blessing of objective and wise friends. On your own, you're making a bet, with lifelong consequences, while in a mind-set that has been proven to be at least somewhat delusional. It's sort of like signing a mortgage or buying a business while drunk. You need to "dry out" a bit and think this thing through before you commit *the rest of your life* to someone you can't objectively evaluate.

Every counselor—indeed, every married person I know—will tell you that it's far better to be lonely and single than lonely and married. The cure for lonely and single is almost always less painful and more hopeful than lonely and married. If you rush into a marital choice and wake up with a difficult coupling, you're going to have to live with some real disappointments. The Bible doesn't give us an "oops, I acted too hastily" clause when it comes to marriage and divorce.

How foolish it would be to let a neurochemical reaction guaranteed to fade in a matter of months lead you to make a lifelong decision. How equally foolish to insist on a short-term neurochemical reaction to consider a lifelong decision. Is it possible you've neglected getting to know some very fine marriage partners, simply because the initial romantic attachment wasn't strong enough? Are you staying with someone who isn't good for you, only because the romantic thrill makes it so hard to leave?

Let me put this in another context. Let's say that I, as a man married twenty-eight years, "fall in love" with someone other than my wife. Would you say that's reason enough for me to divorce my wife and pursue a romantic relationship with another woman?

I hope not.

But if "falling in love" shouldn't direct my actions as a married man, why should it direct your actions as a single? Don't just say that the mere absence of a prior commitment is what renders an infatuation moot. You've already agreed, by my example, that infatuation isn't an absolute indicator of what we should or shouldn't do. Your commitment to "seek first the kingdom of God" should be every bit as strong as my commitment to my marital vows. If an infatuation would compromise that prior commitment, you dare not follow it.

I'm trying to get you to see that falling in love, even as a single, is something to evaluate, not something you should slavishly give yourself over to. "Falling in love" is what it is—a very pleasant, very real brain obsession—but it's a dangerous and false god.

STUDY QUESTIONS

1. Describe your first infatuation (if you've had one). Was there a second or third infatuation? In hindsight, do you think the person(s) you became infatuated with was worthy of your romantic attention?

2. Can you relate to what researchers call the "idealization" of someone—giving them qualities they don't really have, and being blinded to weaknesses? What can people do to protect themselves against this?

3. Have feelings ever led you into a relationship that never should have started? Have the lack of feelings ever led you to end a relationship that should have been given more time? What role do you want romantic feelings to play in future relationships?

4. Have you ever known someone (perhaps yourself) who got into a romantic relationship with a psychologically unhealthy person? How did it end (or what are they dealing with now)? What can this teach you about entering into future relationships?

5. What do you believe is a reasonable time frame for two people to progress from meeting each other to becoming engaged? What do you base this on?

4

YOU DON'T WANT WHAT
YOU THINK YOU WANT

Let me talk to the women first, and then the guys. However, I'd like both genders to read both sections so that you can consider the weight of all that I'm suggesting here. Part of finding the right person to marry is becoming the right person, so take a hint and learn from what I'm telling each gender to avoid.

AN EXCITING MISTAKE

Women, my goal is to get you to care about your boyfriend's godliness as much as a wife cares about her husband's godliness. It's his character that will help keep your life mission alive as feelings begin to fade. I've rarely had a wife complain to me about her husband's looks. When wives send me emails, it's *almost always* about character issues: "He shouldn't do this thing. He should do that thing, but doesn't. How do I fix this?"

Yet most women are not seeking men of character first. They are seeking men with whom they feel "in love." If they do feel in love, they will excuse every fault they see in their man, trying to make the relationship work. If they do not feel in love, they will not seriously consider the man as a potential mate.

Ironically, girlfriends are quick to justify seemingly bad behavior in their boyfriends and try to explain it away, while many wives are eager for everyone around them to know how awful their husbands can be and how everyone should feel sorry for them for having to live with such a wreck of a human being. In fact, not long after they become wives, women will fault men for the very things they overlooked and defended as girlfriends. One woman told counselor Winston Smith, "You don't understand how sick he is! Did I tell you what he did once in college?" Why didn't this episode bother her *before* she got married? Having known this and accepted it, why bring it up now as a wife?

Would that it were the reverse, with girlfriends seriously discussing with their friends their boyfriends' weaknesses so that they could make a wise decision, and wives seriously defending their husbands' honor so that they could make a lasting marriage. Unfortunately, ignoring your boyfriend's weaknesses and gossiping about your husband's failures are two sure paths to divorce.

In front of a very large group, I asked all the married women to stand up. Then I said, "I want you to sit down if you disagree with me that a man's godliness should be one of the top two things a single woman should consider when choosing a mate."

Not one wife—*not one*—sat down. Every married woman was telling every single woman: find a man with solid character who is growing in the Lord and pursuing godliness. That's what those women value most as wives. Yet many single women merely pay lip service to character: "Well, yeah, character and godliness are important, but I think my boyfriend loves God … in his own way."

Too many single women overlook some serious character flaws or maybe even an absence of faith. Because their feelings are so strong, they just can't believe this isn't a match made in heaven. Rather than honestly explore whether this man is worthy of their trust and worthy to become their kids' father, they spend their energy trying to explain away his apparent flaws and to make his spiritual maturity seem acceptable to friends and family members.

Women, ask yourself, what will you most desire in your man ten years from now, when you have kids and a house and are sharing a life together and the infatuation has faded? Find *that*. Look for *that*.

Most married women desire their men to be godly, to have a good sense of humor (life is tough—laughing helps), to be an involved dad, to have a strong work ethic. And yet those four qualities sometimes take a backseat with single women. Some are more attracted to the dreamer who has lots of plans than they are to the workhorse who puts in lots of effort. They value immediate sexual chemistry over a man who keeps his word and lives a respectable life. What so many single women want is a guy who makes their hearts race, their palms sweat, and their sexual chemistry boil, while so many wives want a man they can count on, who will be there for them and their kids every day, and who will faithfully deposit a check in the bank at least once a month.

If you don't deal honestly with this discrepancy—what you value now, and what you'll value ten years from now—you're setting yourself up to live with many regrets. Making a wise marital choice begins with giving proper weight to more significant issues—a shared mission and character traits that will bless you or plague you for the next five or six decades—rather than sexual chemistry or romantic intensity that will fade within months.

It is also easy for women to be carried away by a man's position. Maybe he's wealthy. Maybe he's a leader in the church. So you make assumptions that because he's this or that, everything else must be okay. Here's the thing: you don't marry a *position*. You marry a *person*. Some wealthy guys are stingy. Some ministry guys are jerks. Don't let a guy's position distract you from his person. You're looking for character, not status; you want to find a man who is solid in his core, not just someone who has a solid title.

Can I be blunt? Can I put on my "pastor's hat" here for just a second and flat out tell you what I hope you want? Acts 6:3 sums it up perfectly: "Choose … men … who are known to be full of the Spirit and wisdom." This is what the early church looked for in leaders of their congregations, and it's what you want to look for in leaders of your home. Men who are filled with the Spirit—they are alive to God, and God is active in them—and men who are full of wisdom. You won't regret making a choice founded on *that* basis. Can this honestly be said about your boyfriend? "He's a man full of the Spirit and wisdom"? If not, are you sure you want to settle?

A GORGEOUS MISTAKE

And for you guys—since I'm one of you, I know what you're looking for. We like to look, particularly at gorgeous women. Science has established this (a 2009 Dutch study demonstrated that attractive women can literally derail a man's cognitive functioning[1]), and the Bible concedes this, telling young men in Proverbs 31 not to be led astray by a woman's beauty or charm, because both of these fade. God knows that we are enthralled with physical beauty. One of those Dutch researchers of the study I just referred to—a published, high-degreed professor—met a stunningly beautiful woman at an academic conference. As they talked, he was eager to make a good impression, but when she asked him where he lived, *he literally could not remember his street address.*[2]

Within marriage, this captivation can be a wondrous thing. It's actually a blessing to be enthralled by your wife's breasts (Prov. 5:18–19), but when choosing a wife, we also have to be careful about putting more weight on things that last. In case you've never thought about it, a woman's body changes much more rapidly than her character does.

The same is true of sexual chemistry—what launches sexual chemistry won't sustain sexual chemistry. Your girlfriend might very well be all over you (physically) now, but if you're not married, that in itself is a sign of selfishness: when she wants you, when her libido is high, she's enthusiastic and initiating. But if she loved you, if she genuinely cared for you, she would want what's best for you *in Christ*. She would hold back from inappropriate physical intimacy as she wouldn't want to taunt you or tempt you or pull you away from God.

I can't tell you how many times I've seen this. It's so sad to speak with guys who think their sexually active girlfriends will be sexually active wives just because in the early days of the relationship, when the sexual chemistry was so high, the only problem was reining in the affection, not expressing it. In fact, however, it's almost always the reverse. If your dating relationship is sustained by sin, what will sustain your marriage? If your girlfriend acts selfishly as a girlfriend—wanting sex because she wants it, and wants it now, regardless of whether you're married—why do you think she won't act selfishly as a wife?

The same sin that moves your girlfriend to get *too* physical before marriage is the sin that will kill or perhaps maim sexual intimacy *after* marriage. Sin, by definition, is overturning God's created order. In God's created order, there should be no sex outside of marriage, and lots of fulfilling, generous sex during marriage. Why do you think a person will disobey God in the first instance, but obey Him in the second? Doesn't it make sense that if you shut out God to do what you want to do in one season, you'll keep doing it in the next season?

That's why, when choosing a wife, you want to find a woman who is seeking first God's kingdom *now*. You want to find a woman who is seeking righteousness *now*. If she isn't a mission-based woman while you date, what will make her a mission-based woman after the wedding?

And lest you think that "mission-based woman" sounds boring, puritanical, and even asexual, let me assure you that when it comes to sex, virtue is your *friend*. Find a godly wife who is motivated by God, not just her own desires. God will never stop loving you, God will never stop caring about you, so if a woman is motivated by God and listens to God, she'll keep loving you, too (including sexually), because she'll get that love and motivation from God. And, not to be mean or anything, but there are times when you won't be all that lovable. If your future wife isn't motivated by God, there's not enough about you to keep her interested.

This might shock you, but your best chance at sexual satisfaction in marriage is not to focus on appearance alone, but rather to find a woman of virtue. Proverbs 31 describes her as a woman who "fears the LORD." When a woman is motivated by kindness, compassion, generosity, and understanding; when she is good at forgiving (because I guarantee you, you're going to mess up); when she is desirous to serve as Jesus models service, she's going to be a very satisfying sexual partner and an overall kind wife as well.

I have seen men drool over women who were all but ignored as singles when they hear those women's husbands describe their loving service as wives. These men missed out on some very fine life companions because they were looking for the wrong thing. And I have seen men marry gorgeous women who steadily became less so, and those men made themselves miserable by making such a superficial choice. Proverbs 12:4 warns young men, "A wife of noble character is her husband's crown, but a disgraceful wife is like decay in his bones." If you've ever seen someone slowly waste away of cancer, that phrase—"a disgraceful wife is like decay in his bones"—should strike fear in your heart. You will be eaten from the inside out when you attach yourself to a foolish woman, however beautiful (or rich, or charming) she may be.

Many men I've met have confessed that the reason they are following the Lord so wholeheartedly is because they married a strong Christian woman who wouldn't have married them if they hadn't increased the trajectory of their own spiritual growth. These men frequently confess that they shudder when they think back to what they would have become if they hadn't changed. There might even have been some mixed motives in becoming more serious about the

Lord, but the repentance took, the change has been real, and they feel immeasurably blessed. That's the fruit of hitching yourself to a godly wife who inspires you.

I love being married to a beautiful woman; it's a blessing I won't even try to deny. But I *treasure*, even more, being married to a godly woman.

Here's the reality: many women are led into marriage primarily through romantic idealism, and many men are swept to the altar through sexual attraction. Before you can make a wise marital choice, you have to rid yourself of inferior motivations. The wrong *why* will lead you to the wrong *who*.

FLEETING FUN

Okay, let's compare what the world values with what Jesus teaches. The world values a brief, intense, romantic attraction that makes us both vulnerable and stupid and that lasts, on average, about twelve to eighteen months. It celebrates making rash decisions in a storm of emotion. It evaluates "love" by the intensity of an emotional attachment that science tells us will never really last. In other words, fleeting fun. This is the kind of love celebrated in most movies, novels, television programs, and songs. You've been conditioned to value it above all else and have been told that it's the only "authentic" love.

In *Titanic*, when Rose's new boyfriend says running away together doesn't make any sense (especially since they have known each other for less than seventy-two hours), Rose responds, "It doesn't make any sense. That's why I trust it."[3] While such a philosophy might make for a compelling plot, it almost always creates a grief-ridden life. Such thinking (or, better, *lack* of thinking) has led to many foolish marriages and ruined lives. Romantic infatuation is nice while it lasts, but its impermanence leaves far more pain than its presence ever brought pleasure.

In contrast, Jesus taught us to base our decisions on something eternal: seeking God's kingdom and His righteousness. Jesus's words urge us to find someone with whom we can share a mission instead of an emotional infatuation. Instead of telling us to find someone who makes us lose all sense of objectivity, Jesus's teachings direct us to make a decision that will lead to righteousness—to seek someone who will inspire us toward godliness, who will confront us when we go astray, who will forgive us when we mess up, who can encourage us with wisdom when we are uncertain about how to proceed.

If we are spiritually healthy, this is the life we desire. This is the life that leads to a growing joy, not a fading attachment. The crucial "third stage" of relationship—beyond sexual desire and romantic attachment—is long-term affection. This is a bond that is best fostered through friendship and a shared mission. It lasts until death and, unlike romantic infatuation, gets deeper with age. Time serves intentionally cultivated intimate affection, even as it kills infatuation.

Jesus's words—indeed, the whole of Scripture—call God's people to build a spiritual partnership. That's what you should be looking for: can this person walk with me toward God? It's not selfish to choose wisely in marriage; it's being a good steward of the one life God has given you. If you marry someone with serious mental issues, addictions, or character flaws, it's like entering a marathon with a heavy backpack. Ask yourself, will the person I'm considering help me run the race God has laid out before me, or will they act like an anchor dragging at my feet?

Granted, the marriage choice is different from simply choosing a partner or friend. If there is no sexual attraction, you're going to have a difficult time fulfilling your role as a husband or wife. If the thought of seeing your intended naked makes you want to vomit, don't marry him or her. Sex is a significant aspect of marriage, and if you don't think you can enjoy and enthusiastically participate in sexual relations, you shouldn't get married. In the long term, however, sexual intimacy dies in most marriages due to relational issues more than a lack of physical attraction. Two people who genuinely care for each other, are kind to each other, share a mission together, and want to grow together naturally feel a desire to serve each other, and that includes sexual expression.

Secondly (we'll talk more about this later), never forget that you're also choosing your future kids' mom or dad, so a person's suitability to fulfill that role needs to be taken into consideration. A certain degree of friendship and, yes, compatibility, can foster the maintenance of a spiritual bond. These are all important issues that should be added to the overarching end of a shared spiritual mission.

In other words, there is *more* to think about when choosing a marriage partner than Matthew 6:33 covers, but there should never be *less* than that. If the person you are interested in is not someone with whom you believe you can seek first God's kingdom and pursue a life of righteousness, that's a deal breaker. Never compromise on Matthew 6:33. You need to add to it and build on it, but you ignore it at your peril. It's always more, never less, when it comes to Matthew 6:33 and marriage.

STUDY QUESTION

1. Why do you think the same women who, as girlfriends, often defended their boyfriends, now, as wives, often complain about the same men who have become their husbands? What's going on here?

2. Is it realistic to ask people to consider a person's character above intense romantic feelings? How does one learn to do this?

3. Gary suggested that most women end up desiring a godly husband who has a good sense of humor, who is an involved dad, and who has a strong work ethic, but that single women are often drawn to the "dreamers" with whom they have a strong sexual chemistry. Women, do you think there are any discrepancies between what you'll desire in a husband and the kind of guy who interests you as a boyfriend? Discuss these.

4. Given that men are biologically predisposed to be impressed with physical beauty, how can they base the decision to marry on a woman's qualities that will outlast physical appearance? Is this question even realistic to ask?

5. Compare and contrast what the world typically values in romantic relationships and what the Bible suggests makes up true and lasting love.

5

SOUL MATE OR SOLE MATE?

The young woman calling the radio program admitted that the man she was dating was—for lack of a better word—a jerk. He had cheated on her with her best friend, he had no aspirations, and any objective person could see that the guy she had fallen for was not suitable marriage material. Still, she persisted in her devotion: "I know I can't trust him, I know he doesn't treat me very well, I know he's not going anywhere—but ... but ... I think he may be *the one*."

She recognized marrying him would be a disaster because, frankly, *dating* him had been a disaster. But if you believe there's only one right person for you, and that person just happens to be a selfish loser, what else are you supposed to do?

Our culture has widely embraced the notion that there is just one person who can, in the words immortalized by Tom Cruise in *Jerry Maguire*, "complete us." This is a perilous mind-set with which to approach a lifelong marital decision, even though it is the majority opinion. Studies show that most singles are in a somewhat desperate search for their "soul mate." One Rutgers University study found that 94 percent of single women in their twenties say that the first requirement in a spouse is that he's a soul mate, someone with whom they feel an almost cosmic connection. Just as surprising, 87 percent think they'll actually find that person "when they are ready."

BLAME ZEUS

The origins of this "soul mate" line of thinking are so bizarre you'll hardly believe it, but it's worthwhile to delve into a tiny bit of philosophy to expose a line of thinking that so many people today adopt without even really thinking about it. Well over two thousand years ago, the Greek philosopher Plato surmised that there was once a "super race" of androgynous humans that made an attempt to overthrow the gods. This super race consisted of "round" people, comprising both male and female in one person, and in that state they were getting too powerful, so Zeus said, "I shall now cut each of them in two, … and they will be both weaker and more useful to us through the increase in their numbers."[1]

The forceful cutting in two supposedly left both halves desperate to be reunited. When the two halves did finally find each other, all they could do was cling to each other, which led to their deaths "because they were unwilling to do anything apart from one another."[2] Zeus saved the day—deprived and desperate humans are no longer so powerful and no longer such a threat to the gods.

Notice, however, that in Plato's view, romantic love makes us weaker, whereas in the biblical view, love makes us stronger. What is your love doing to you—are you stronger in the midst of it, or do you feel more vulnerable, weak, and perhaps even desperate?

Infatuation can lead us down the path of desperation, can't it? You feel so connected to someone that you can't bear to be apart, even for a few hours. You feel vulnerable in a whole new way. Life apart from the relationship feels so unimportant that it virtually stops. Well, Plato figured that's because there was a time when you *weren't* apart and therefore can't function on your own.

He went on to suggest,

> So it is really from such early times that human beings have had, inborn in themselves, Eros for one another—Eros, the bringer-together of their ancient nature [i.e., man and woman as one being], who tries to make one out of two and to heal their human nature. Each of us, then, is a token of a human being, because we are sliced like fillets of sole, two out of one; and so each is always in search of his own token.[3]

This is the philosophical foundation of the "soul mate"—finding your lost half.

TRUE HUMAN NATURE

A scriptural view of human nature couldn't be more different. According to the Bible, our problem is not that we've been sliced apart from an ancient human half, but that we have been separated from God by our sin and need to be reconciled to God through the work of Jesus Christ on the cross. Once we are reconciled to God, He brings us together as humans. Marriage is a wonderful, even glorious reality, but it is secondary to our spiritual identity as children of God and something that won't even exist in heaven (Matt. 22:30).

Our search for a life mate, then, isn't one of desperation, but rather one of patiently looking for someone with whom we can share God's love and live out God's purpose.

Plato's "soul mate" philosophy circumvents the concept of applying wisdom and replaces it with trying to mystically discern whether you are "meant to be" with someone. For every person who stumbles into a sensible matching with this guidance, there are a dozen who act foolishly and hastily. For starters, how do you know if someone is your destined soul mate? Most typically, people try to discern it through their feelings. They sense a connection unlike anything they've ever known before. But we've already established that infatuation is powerful, all-consuming—*and short-lived.*

Some well-meaning believers might try to say, "I asked God," and while I applaud your pursuit of heavenly guidance, can I at least question your objectivity and ability to discern God's voice when your brain is obsessed with getting and keeping someone with whom you've fallen into a deep infatuation?

Discerning someone's character, true values, and suitability for marriage is *hard work.* It takes time, counsel, and a healthy dose of objective self-doubt and skepticism. Identifying someone as "God's chosen" or Plato's "soul mate" is comparatively easy. You "feel" it in your gut. It *seems* right. You can't imagine anyone else. You must have found *the one!*

Such individuals marry on an infatuation binge without seriously considering character, compatibility, life goals, family desires, spiritual health, and other important concerns. Then when the infatuation fades and the relationship requires work, one or both partners suddenly discover that they were "mistaken." This person must not be their soul mate after all; otherwise, it wouldn't be so much work. Next, they panic. Their soul mate must still be out there! Such people can't get to divorce court fast enough, lest someone steal their "one true soul mate" meant only for them.

The sad reality is that when we get married for trivial reasons, we will seek divorce for trivial reasons. We need something much more lasting on which to base a lifelong commitment—one that even has eternal implications.

Let me ask you a tough question: if someone is willing to marry you without doing the hard work of determining whether you're suitable to be their spouse and their future kids' parent, what makes you think they'll do the hard work of building a satisfying, God-honoring marriage? The *way* someone chooses to get married is a good indicator of the work they'll put in after the wedding takes place in order to make the marriage grow. If someone cuts corners in the decision process—willing to risk their own *and your* happiness on something as precarious as an infatuation—how do you know they won't want to cut corners when it comes to the nitty-gritty work of building marital intimacy stitch by stitch?

ARE YOU TRYING TO REPLACE GOD?

Take a deep breath. Your marital choice is crucial, but it will *never* define you. If you are a believer, God—not your marital status (or marital happiness or frustration)—defines your life. Don't put too much pressure on yourself. Let the pursuit of marriage be one of joy, one you undertake with your closest eternal companion—God Himself—walking with you.

You're not trying to replace God by finding your perfect match—that's desperation. You are already perfectly loved and looking for someone who can help you grow in and share that love—that's security. Christians should never be defined by the word *desperate*. We are well loved, well cared for, adored by the One who knows us best, and secure in His acceptance, love, affirmation, and purpose.

On the other hand, while it can be a tremendous ego boost to have someone seem like they are desperate for you, ask yourself if you're willing to play the role of God in their life. One young woman once told me (when I was single), "I could never be happy without you." When I talked this over with my campus pastor, he helped me see that this was a red flag. It initially felt nice to be so wanted and needed, but he explained how someone who says this of another human being isn't in a right relationship with God. Did I want to join my future with someone who allowed God to have such a small role in her life that another fallen human would forever determine her happiness?

Before we can go on, you need to wrestle with this question: do you believe there is only one right person to marry? Perhaps you reject Plato's soul-mate line of thinking but have developed a "Christian alternative," something along the lines of finding the one person whom God created "just for you."

If so, how do you justify that biblically? Let's look at the evidence.

YOU'RE A REGENT: LEARN TO ACT LIKE ONE

The language of the Bible doesn't suggest there is one right choice for marriage. Rather, all the teaching passages seem to suggest that there are wise and unwise choices. We are encouraged to use wisdom, not destiny, as our guide when choosing a marital partner.

Proverbs takes a supremely pragmatic approach: "A wife of noble character *who can find*?" (31:10). This verse assumes that we are involved in a serious pursuit, actively engaging our minds to make a wise choice. And the top thing a young man should consider is this: "Charm is deceptive, and beauty is fleeting; but a woman who fears the LORD is to be praised" (Prov. 31:30). The Bible tells young men to search for a woman of character; it reminds these men that while looks won't last, godly character improves with age. It says nothing—absolutely nothing—about "feelings." It even warns against putting too much emphasis on physical attraction or social grace. Instead, *this verse makes a woman's faith the defining characteristic of her suitability to be an excellent wife.*

I can speak from experience: nothing compares to being married to a godly woman—nothing! Kindness, generosity, spiritual companionship—these all grow deeper and truer and more pleasant over time. But I know from counseling far too many troubled marriages that there is also nothing more tedious and exhausting than being married to a stunningly beautiful but narcissistic woman.

You can take this too far; as I already stated, I'm not suggesting you marry someone in whom you have no sexual interest at all. But the first priority, according to Scripture, is to find a spiritually compatible person, and *then,* under *that* umbrella, find a *sexually* compatible person. If you reverse those two categories, you can expect to find short-term satisfaction at the risk of long-term frustration. Let the "why" of marriage point you to the "who," and don't let a stunningly beautiful "who" change your reason "why." (And if you are blessed to find an awesomely godly and amazingly beautiful person, all wrapped up in one, you are blessed indeed.)

When we jump forward to the New Testament, there is no hint at all about finding "the one person" that God created "just for you." It's far more a pragmatic choice: do you think you'll sin sexually if you don't get married (1 Cor. 7:2)? Are you acting improperly toward a woman you could marry (1 Cor. 7:36)? If so, go ahead and get married—it's your choice, and God gives you that freedom. But notice this: the choice is made *on the basis of seeking righteousness.* "Do you think you might keep sinning if you stay single? Then get married."

In helping people wrestle with the decision to marry, the apostle Paul admitted that there are benefits to singleness (particularly in the historical context out of which he's writing to the Corinthians) and benefits to being married. If you're unable to handle sexual temptation as a single, Paul said, then by all means get married. This is, blatantly, an admonition to base a marital decision on the desire to live a more righteous life, knowing that without marriage you might fall into unrighteous living.

Notice 1 Corinthians 7:8–9. Paul also left the decision *whether* to get married up to us: "Now to the unmarried and the widows I say: It is good for them to stay unmarried, as I am. But if they cannot control themselves, they should marry."

Paul was simply modeling the pragmatic approach of Jesus, who spoke matter-of-factly about people who were born eunuchs (that is, able to live a satisfying life without ever becoming sexually active) and others who "choose to live like eunuchs for the sake of the kingdom of heaven" (Matt. 19:12 NIV 2011). Did you get that word *choose*? Jesus says it's a *choice*. It is not wrong if you want to get married; it is not wrong to want to stay single. The Bible clearly says we shouldn't feel forced to marry or feel prohibited from marrying; this is one of those life decisions God leaves up to us. But God *does* care about *why* we decide to marry and the kind of person we marry.

The crowning piece of our argument, however, the one the "Christian Platonists" are going to have a difficult time overcoming, is Paul's advice in 1 Corinthians 7:39, where Paul clearly left the choice of marriage up to us in the clearest, most explicit of terms: "She is free to marry anyone she wishes, but he must belong to the Lord." Did you catch that? *She is free to marry anyone she wishes* as long as the man she "wishes" belongs to the Lord. Could Scripture be any clearer?

Scripture thus tells us that it is our choice *whether* we want to get married and *who* we want to marry. In other words, *you get to choose*. This isn't a denial of God's providence, nor does it preclude God leading two people together in certain cases. Rather, it's the Bible's way of saying that while marriage is really important, it's also something God lets us decide whether we want to be participants in, and who we want to be participants with. God has given you an awesome responsibility, so choose wisely.

The lazy and overly mystical might resent this teaching. They might say, "That's not fair, God—just tell me who to marry, and

I'll get married." That's an immature attitude. God created both men and women to be ruling agents (Gen. 1:28), and as redeemed Christians, we will rule again in eternity (1 Cor. 6:2–3). The ability to rule is something we grow into, and marriage is a golden opportunity to develop the discernment and discretion we need to become fully functioning regents in God's kingdom work.

The need to find "the one" is based in desperation—as if, apart from that "one," we lack something. The Bible views us as recipients of God's perfect love, already charged with an important life mission (seeking first the kingdom of God), and thus the decision to marry, though crucial, won't define us. Nor will *who* we marry define us. It's sort of like this: medical wisdom says you need to exercise and eat right to be at your best. How you exercise—whether you ride a bike, swim, or jog—is really up to you. Just exercise. The Bible says we need to live a righteous life, including how we handle our sexual and emotional desires, seeking first the kingdom of God above all else. How we do that—whether as singles or marrieds, whether pursuing an introverted bookworm or an extroverted jock to be our life partner—is up to us.

In all honesty, this is a check on a secular culture that makes too much of marriage. The warning behind this reality is that if we make too much of marriage, we make too little of our relationship with God. And when we make too little of our relationship with God, we undercut our source of love, which makes success in marriage less likely. Focusing on marriage too much is, ironically enough, the best way to kill it.

Men and women, find a partner with whom you can seek first the kingdom of God, someone who inspires you toward righteousness, and when you do, "all these things will be added to you."

MAKING THE CHOICE

The reason it is so crucial to adopt the Bible's view of a wise choice over "finding the one" is that the former attitude allows you to objectively consider the person you marry. There is no objective measurement of "destiny." How, indeed, can you possibly know if someone is your soul mate? Powerful emotions can blind us to all sorts of clues. But when we adopt the biblical attitude of making a wise choice, we can use all that God has given us to arrive at a solid decision that should be based on a number of factors:

- Scriptural Mandates
  Is the person a believer who fears God (Prov. 31:30) and who is biblically eligible for marriage (Mark 10:11–12)?
- Wisdom
  How do they handle their money (Prov. 31:16, 18)?
  Is this person a hard worker (Prov. 13:4; 26:13–15)?
  Do they live an upright life (Prov. 13:6, 20; 25:28)?
  Does this person wound people with their words, or are they an encourager (Prov. 12:18; 18:21)?
  Are they peaceful, or are they quarrelsome (Prov. 17:19; 29:8)?
- Parental and Pastoral Advice
  Your parents know you better than you may realize, and even if they aren't believers, they still usually want the best for you. At least consider their opinions. Also talk to your pastor and other

godly people you respect: "Does this relationship seem like a 'fit' to you? Are there any areas you're concerned about?"

Proverbs 15:22 tells us, "Plans fail for lack of counsel, but with many advisers they succeed." If the people I most respect had serious reservations about a relationship, I would assume I had lost my objectivity—that I was both vulnerable and stupid due to infatuation—and put all marriage plans on hold.

- Prayer

Rejecting the notion that God creates one person just for us doesn't discount the reality that God can lead us toward someone and help us make a wise choice when we seek Him in prayer. We want to surrender to God's providence by seeking and using the gift of wisdom, applied learning, and rational understanding.

Grappling with all of the above may not sound romantic, but it is not antiromance. It's entirely possible to become infatuated with someone whom you would be very wise to marry. The difference is, you're not marrying them *because* you're infatuated with them. And, hopefully, you're not completely discounting other possibilities simply because you're *not* infatuated with them.

Instead of a "soul mate," I'd like to suggest a more biblical pursuit. It sounds exactly the same, but the meaning is radically different. You need to look for a "sole mate."

WHAT IS A SOLE MATE?

A sole mate is someone who walks out with us (the "sole" of a shoe!) the biblical command to seek first the kingdom of God. This is all about the shoe-leather application of biblical love. The most accurate definition of true love is found in John 15:13: "Greater love has no one than this, that he lay down his life for his friends."

This love isn't based on feelings; it's based on sacrifice. The Bible calls men to act like martyrs toward their wives, laying down their own lives on their wives' behalf (Eph. 5:25). Titus says older women need to train younger women how to love their husbands (Titus 2:4). Need I point out, men and women, that these are *severe* verses, to an extreme? Martyrdom on behalf of your wife? Being "trained"— actively studying and learning—how to love your husband? This is heavy stuff. Guys, you may feel infatuated now, but in agreeing to become a husband of one wife, you are agreeing to put her needs above your own for the rest of your life—regardless of what happens. Are you ready for that? And women, as soon as you say "I do," you are committing before God and the community of faith to expend your best efforts helping, loving, and supporting this man. Infatuation fills your eyes with what you're *getting*, but let the Bible fill your mind with what you're committing to *give*.

These passages alone are enough to tell us that within marriage, love is not an emotion; it's a policy and a commitment that we choose to keep in the harshest of circumstances. It's something that can be learned and that we can grow in. Biblical love is not based on the worthiness of the person being loved—none of us deserves Christ's sacrifice—but on the worthiness of the One who calls us to love: "We love because he first loved us" (1 John 4:19).

Christian life is a journey toward love, growing in love, expanding in our ability to love, surrendering our hearts to love, increasingly becoming a person who is motivated by love. A "sole mate" appreciates that marriage is a partnership committed to the task of walking out the biblical mandate to always put love first. It's not marked by the couple who displays the most emotion, with the biggest smiles on their faces, who can't keep their hands off each other; but rather, the women or men who, through the duties and sacrifice of marriage, have trained themselves to love with God's love. They walk out the gospel on a daily basis, forgiving, serving, and putting others first in the most ordinary issues of life in such a way that they see themselves in training for godliness. Such a couple will grow together, as surely as merely sentimental couples will grow apart.

A biblical sole mate who walks in this truth, who daily travels God's journey of sacrificial love, and who willingly goes "into training" for godliness is a far more stable foundation upon which to build a lifelong partnership than the thought of the philosopher Plato. "Greater love has no one than this: to lay down one's life for one's friends" (John 15:13 NIV 2011). This may not sound like the most *exciting* or *emotional* love, but it is certainly the *truest* love. And it is the only kind of love that lasts.

STUDY QUESTIONS

1. Having read this chapter, do you believe there is just one person you're "supposed" to marry? What do you base this belief on? How will this affect the way you approach finding a marriage partner?

2. Discuss this statement: "Notice, however, that in Plato's view, romantic love makes us weaker, whereas in the biblical view, love makes us stronger." Compare that with your own experience.

3. Do you think the *way* someone chooses to get married (in a rush, without due diligence, or deliberately and with counsel) might reflect whether they will put in the relational work necessary to make a marriage succeed and continue to grow ever more intimate throughout the years? Why or why not?

4. Why is it dangerous to date when you feel desperate? How can someone deal with such desperation responsibly so that it doesn't affect who they choose to marry?

5. Do you agree that the mystical approach of asking God to just tell you who you "should" marry is an immature way to approach getting married? Why or why not?

6. How might the "sole mate" notion of love—marriage being designed not to complete us, but to provide us with a life partner with whom we can grow in our ability to love—affect who you consider marrying?

6

A MATCH MADE IN HEAVEN?

ISAAC AND REBEKAH

As soon as I tell people that we shouldn't assume God has chosen one person just for us, they usually say, "What about Isaac and Rebekah?" This is a tremendous love story, and worthy of some consideration, so let's spend a little time looking at it to determine what the Bible really does teach through this famous love story.

To bring those of you who haven't read the story up to date, in Genesis 24 we read that Abraham sent his servant to find a suitable wife for his son Isaac. Abraham was getting old and increasingly concerned that his son didn't have a wife. Without a wife, there could be no heir, and a lot of very important promises hinged on Isaac producing an heir. Accordingly, Abraham pulled his servant aside and gave him the task of finding a suitable wife for Isaac. Essentially, to keep the faith/racial bloodline pure, Abraham wanted Isaac to marry a Jewish woman, not a Canaanite. Right away, we see the limitations of using this motivation in New Testament times, but let's move on from that.

Abraham's servant prayed for success: "O LORD, the God of my master Abraham, please grant me success today, and show loving-kindness to my master Abraham" (Gen. 24:12 NASB).

This is the *first* time in Scripture that we read of someone asking God for specific guidance. From all the rest of Scripture, we naturally assume that part of prayer is seeking guidance, but this is the first recorded instance of prayer being used in that way. And *this first recorded instance seeks guidance for making a wise marital choice.*

From this we can deduce that it is not wise to reduce the marital decision-making process to reason alone. Wise decision making is to be applauded, but it is entirely appropriate to seek God's discernment, to listen to His voice, to let Him give us some feedback on our inclinations. We may get no confirmation or warning—but it is wise to give God an opportunity to do just that. Certainly, as in all important decisions, we should adopt an attitude of prayer and ask others to pray for us as well.

KIND WOMEN ONLY NEED APPLY

Look not only at the fact that Abraham's servant prayed but also at *what* he prayed for:

> Behold, I am standing by the spring, and the
> daughters of the men of the city are coming out to
> draw water; now may it be that the girl to whom I
> say, "Please let down your jar so that I may drink,"

and who answers, "Drink, and I will water your camels also"—may she be the one whom You have appointed for Your servant Isaac; and by this I will know that You have shown lovingkindness to my master. (vv. 13–14 NASB)

The "charismatic" way to read this is to suggest that the woman's response was neutral except to serve as a sign: this would be the one God had chosen because she was saying the right words. Go back and read those words again. Another way to understand them is that Abraham's servant asked God to let the woman He had chosen be the kind of woman who was described in this prayer ("may she be the one …"). Such a woman would have had to be extraordinarily generous and kind. Each camel could drink up to *twenty-five gallons of water.* Asking God to choose a woman who was willing to draw up that much extra water, for *ten* camels, when the water had to be pulled up (there were no "faucets" on a well), on the heels of a comparatively minor request (one man's thirst), is tantamount to hitchhiking for a ride and asking God to lead the driver to offer to take you cross-country. Such a woman's response would be abnormally generous, well beyond the bounds of common civility and certainly way beyond any cultural expectations of hospitality.[1]

Abraham's servant wasn't just asking for a sign; he was asking for a woman of character who would be one in a thousand. He clearly wanted his master's son to have a wife who would bless him with hospitality, so he wanted a woman who would go well above a simple request. The Bible praises Rebekah's beauty and purity (v. 16), but the servant was seeking a woman who was uncommonly kind and generous. That's what he wanted for Isaac.

And that's exactly what we've been talking about: find that person whose character shines above all others.

A CHOSEN FAMILY

In this instance, the most natural reading of Scripture is that God had chosen one woman, Rebekah, to be Isaac's wife. But when applying this to your own life, consider the following: God's purpose in establishing a union between Isaac and Rebekah required her to be of a certain nationality. That is no longer the case for us when choosing whom to marry (Gal. 3:28). Instead, we are instructed to find a person of a common *faith*. Furthermore, Abraham's family was specially chosen to bless the entire earth; while we are also chosen to build God's kingdom, Isaac's pure bloodline and place in history was a special calling, unique to his bloodline, particularly as it related to producing certain heirs. New Testament reproduction isn't about blood*lines*, but rather blood *application* (the cross of Christ).

Also keep in mind, Old Testament narratives aren't always normative. The Old Testament describes what happened, but that doesn't mean we should copy what happens, especially since the Old Testament isn't always explicit about denouncing clearly inappropriate actions. While God clearly blessed the union of David and Bathsheba with the birth of Solomon, it would be a monstrosity of application to suggest that adultery and then a covered-up murder is an acceptable method for meeting and choosing a mate. Likewise, no one would suggest that a widow should search for a man twice her age, work in his field, and uncover the man's feet in the middle of the night to offer marriage, as Ruth did. Yet, indisputably, these became significant unions and families in the genealogy leading up to the birth of the Christ.

In other words, the story of Isaac and Rebekah is an account of what was, but not necessarily of what should be for all of God's people. Just because there may have been one ordained wife for Isaac doesn't mean there is one ordained wife for *you.* Of course, in your case it's entirely possible that God may have a woman He particularly desires you to marry. It is certainly within a reasonable understanding of God's working through history to believe that He can create and call two people together under His providence to accomplish a particular work. But even if that's the case in your life, how can you discern such a calling? I believe the wise response is to apply everything we've been talking about. That's how God's call is discerned. To *presume* on God's call, or to confuse infatuation with God's call, is as foolish as ignoring God's call altogether.

What I see happening most often is that people seek "God's will" primarily as a shortcut. They don't want to do the hard work of finding and testing out a suitable mate, so they seek a mystical or emotional sign that "this is the one." Friends, that's foolish. Mystical leadings and emotional connections are confusing at best and a deplorable foundation on which to base a monumental decision.

This is not to suggest that God doesn't occasionally work "outside the box"—I'm being as balanced as I can be here. For example, it was clearly God's will for Joseph to take Mary as his wife (Matt. 1:20–25). If God appears to you in a dream and says that He is fulfilling prophecies through your future marital union, and you can be sure that it really is God speaking, friend, marry that person!

But I seriously doubt that God will give most of us such a certain and extremely specific direction. According to the full account of Scripture, for the vast majority of us, whether we marry, and whom we marry, falls under God's permissive will.

Thus, if you will keep reading, we will continue the work of helping to equip you to make a supremely *wise* marital choice.

STUDY QUESTIONS

1. The start of Isaac and Rebekah's story teaches us to cover the process of choosing a mate with prayer. How big a role has prayer played in your own pursuit? Do you need to increase this in any way?

2. How can the *content* of Abraham's servant's prayer—searching for an extraordinarily kind partner for his master's son—direct our own prayers for a future spouse?

3. If someone truly believes that God is calling them to marry a *particular* person, what are some reasonable tests of that calling?

4. How can the story of Isaac and Rebekah direct our own marital pursuit? In what ways is the story *not* relevant for today's believers?

7

THE RELIGIOUS
ROMANCE LOTTERY

"When it comes to choosing a mate, God will bring the right person to me at the right time. I'll just sit back and wait."

That sounds so spiritual, so trusting, so … holy.

But consider this attitude in virtually any other aspect of life. For instance, how "holy" and wise does this sound: "I don't plan to apply to any colleges. I figure if I'm supposed to go to college, God will make sure the University of Texas sends me a letter, complete with a dorm key. That'll be my sign."

Or this: "Why should I fill out any job applications? If God wants me to work at Microsoft, He can have the CEO give me a call."

If someone spoke like that, you'd think that person was a verifiable religious fanatic. But we put the language of dating and finding a mate into similar "Christianese," and it sounds so noble: "Don't worry about finding someone to marry. If you just focus on God, He'll bring someone along at just the right time."

There are some very disappointed people in their thirties who lived by this philosophy and now fight resentment toward God because they still aren't married. After all, wasn't He supposed to bring their future spouse to their doorstep?

Just as bad, many people show open disdain for anyone who goes to college in part hoping to find someone to marry or who even seems intentional in their pursuit. I'm a firm believer in a good education, but let's be honest: most people will never use the degree they get from college. That doesn't mean the degree and experience of learning aren't valuable—they certainly are—but the person you marry will have a far greater impact on your life satisfaction than your major (or lack of one, if you choose not to go to college) ever will. What's so wrong with spending four years trying to find a suitable life mate—perhaps not as the main goal of college, but certainly one of the top goals? Or, if you're not a college student, what's wrong with attending a church that offers many opportunities to meet eligible men and women your age? It's not like there's only one right church to attend, and if marriage is an honorable estate, and one church gives you a better opportunity to enter that estate, well, you could base your choice for a church on worse things than that. If I'm looking for a job, I'm going to go to job fairs. If I'm looking for a mate, I'm going to look in places where I'm likely to find more options.

Some women are cautious, believing (with some good reasoning) that they want a man to pursue *them*. What I'm suggesting doesn't contradict that; however, are you putting yourself in situations where you can be pursued? Are you in a place where you can be noticed? Can you do anything to put yourself in somebody's mind-set?

If you've got a group of girlfriends and want to let some guys know you exist, the answer is so easy: it's called "food." Throw a party. Feed the guys. They'll figure out who put the food on the table.

WALK TOWARD THE MUSIC

My wife and I arrived in Baden-Baden, Germany, late on a summer evening. Our hotel sat in the midst of a pedestrian district that, except for a couple restaurants and gelato parlors, practically shut down by 8:00 p.m. We weren't ready to call it a night and wondered what we should do.

In the distance, I could just make out the faint sound of some music. "Hey," I suggested, "let's walk toward the music. Something must be going on."

Sure enough, there was. An outdoor concert serenaded twelve to fifteen makeshift restaurants just outside Baden-Baden's famous casino, welcoming the tourists who were there for the horse races that weekend. Apparently, one of the reasons the pedestrian area was drained of all activity was because the concert had sucked everybody over there.

"Walking toward the music" isn't a bad philosophy of life. Doors might seem closed, the evening might seem prematurely over, but if you can catch a glimpse of nightlife or hear the sound of music in the distance, why not walk toward it and see what you find?

Some Christians find themselves in a dating dead end. There's no one suitable where they work or at their church. For their own reasons, they refuse to look at any online dating sites. Instead of putting themselves in social environments where they might find someone, they start to feel bitter and angry and blame God for not bringing the right one along.

Your passivity is not God's fault. *Walk toward the music.* See what you find. Become proactive, intentional, and even energetic about finding someone to marry. When God, through Scripture, asks young men, "A wife of noble character who can find?" (Prov. 31:10), the entire assumption is that such a pursuit involves a serious search.

Studies and personal experience reveal that most people find their eventual mate at church or work or are introduced through family and friends. A growing number are signing up for an online matchmaking service. These are all solid avenues to explore.

Are you putting yourself in places where you can find or be found? Do you hang out in places where the kind of person you want to marry hangs out? The reason my son chose the college he did was because, on his visit, he discovered that the students he met there were the kind of people he wanted to hang around for four years. If you can't change your work environment, you *can* change your social calendar or where you exercise.

In other words, just because it's difficult to find someone, don't just go back to your hotel room and call it a night. Walk toward the music. Catch a glimpse of possibility, and make the effort.

LAZY IN LOVE

My friend Steve Watters has wisely said, "People who marry well aren't lucky in love. They're intentional in their path." Too many Christians are lazy in love—expecting God to make up for their sloth.

When we view getting married as an intentional pursuit, and if we accept the premise that there isn't just one person you can be happily married to, we can draw the following conclusions:

- Instead of simply "waiting for God to bring the right one," go out and find a godly mate. That's what God specifically tells us to do in Proverbs 31:10. It's even what Abraham sent his servant to do on behalf of Isaac.

- Choose social situations where you are more likely to meet a diverse number of people who qualify as acceptable marriage partners.

- In the face of sexual temptation, increase your odds of marrying well by getting more serious about pursuing marriage, in part by focusing on your own character—spiritually, financially, relationally, and emotionally. Taking sexual shortcuts hinders a healthy marriage and delays a holy solution.

- Do what you can to make yourself more attractive as a marriage partner. Learn how to hold your own in a conversation. Don't go heavily into debt. If you need to get in shape, do so. "Waiting on God" can be a cop-out if you're not working on yourself. Maybe God's waiting on you to get your house in order.

- Laziness never honors God. The Bible is brutal when denouncing sloth. If you put off a serious pursuit of marriage, if you deny the need to keep yourself in good shape, don't blame God when you reap the consequences of your own actions.

- While pursuing marriage is a good and holy pursuit, it shouldn't become the primary pursuit.

We are told to seek *first* the kingdom of God, not seek first marriage. So don't put your faith, worship, and service on a shelf, assuming you can pick it back up once you find your mate.

Finding a wonderful life mate is not about winning the lottery. It's not a mystical exercise. This isn't to suggest you shouldn't seek God's guidance and make your choice prayerfully—of course you should—but in the end, you're making a rational, biblically informed, and hopefully wisely counseled choice. Own it—both the process *and* the final decision.

STUDY QUESTIONS

1. Have you ever (or do you now) believed the opening statement of this chapter: "When it comes to choosing a mate, God will bring the right person to me at the right time. I'll just sit back and wait"? After reading this chapter, have your thoughts changed at all?
2. Are there any ways in which you can begin walking toward the music?
3. Since studies show most people eventually find their mate at church or work, or are introduced through family and friends, what can you do in the coming months to more earnestly pursue a marriage partner through these avenues?
4. What things might you need to address or improve in your own life in order to be seen as someone that a person would truly want to marry?

8

PASSIVE SURRENDER OR PASSIONATE PURSUIT?

COMPELLING REASONS TO GET MARRIED

As soon as you put away the notion that there's "one right person" to marry, you can apply wisdom; and wisdom says if you're struggling sexually, it's time to be even more aggressive about finding a suitable spouse. God will honor your motivation. In fact, putting off such a pursuit can be spiritually reckless and morally dangerous.

Even if you disagree with what I've just said, I think you'll agree with these three points:

1. God designed most of us to get married. A few may be called to celibacy, but statistically, over 90 percent of us will experience marriage at least once in our lives.

2. You'll never have a larger pool to draw from for a suitable, godly marriage partner than during your university years, or if you attend a large church with an active singles group. Don't be ashamed of using this opportunity.

3. God made you a sexual being but commands you to restrict sexual activity to marriage (1 Cor. 6:15–20; 7:36–38; 1 Thess. 4:3–7). At a certain point, for some of you it will become overwhelmingly difficult, to the point of courting temptation, to delay the marriage that will allow a holy expression of sexual activity.

Though the average age for a man to get married in this country is now twenty-eight, and the average age for a woman is approaching twenty-seven, the fact is, you've been created by God with a body that is ready for sexual activity a decade before that. (I don't believe most eighteen-year-olds are ready for marriage—but hang with me here.) A cavalier attitude toward this disconnect can result in premarital sexual sin that dishonors God and threatens your integrity as well as your future sexual satisfaction in marriage.

SEXUAL DESIRE: A MOTIVATION TO MARRY?

A young college student once dismissed the biblical teaching that God restricts all sexual activity to marriage as "unrealistic."

"The fact that God made us as sexual beings does mean something," I replied, "and in most cases it means young people should get married much sooner than they do."

"So are you saying that the desire to be sexually active is a good enough reason to get married?"

Few people today would question the motivation of a young couple who proclaimed, "We want to get married because we are head over heels in love," even though what they are experiencing is a flood of neuropeptides that neurologists tell us will not and cannot last longer than twelve to eighteen months. Sexual need and desire, however, will be a constant for at least the next four or five decades, if not more. Why is it nobler to base a lifelong decision on a relatively temporary emotional disposition and disregard a God-designed motivation that may never fade? Not *once* does the Bible say, "If you're out of your mind with infatuation, by all means, get married!" But it *does* say, "It is better to marry than to burn with passion [or sexual desire]" (1 Cor. 7:9 NASB).

We Christians—believing in God as Creator—should be the *last* ones to discount the delight and pleasure of sexuality *or* the need to respect God's design for this relationship to take place within a lifelong commitment. In fact, we honor God when we submit to the call to marriage. Marriage is God's creation, and we should surrender to it as part of our worship. If sexual temptation isn't even an issue in your life, these words don't apply to you. But if you are pretending to believe in sexual purity yet still leaving behind you a wake of sexual casualties, demonstrating that you are particularly weak in this area and likely to keep falling, you're fooling yourself by pretending otherwise. Not only are you hurting others, but you're developing attitudes and habits toward sexuality that will hinder sexual satisfaction within marriage and become a burden to your future spouse.

CULTURAL CONDITIONING

Those of you who may be struggling with sexual temptation but are still insisting on a romantic "storm of emotion" before you get married should at least realize that you've been culturally conditioned to think this way.

Dr. Hsu, a Chinese anthropologist, wrote, "An American asks, 'How does my heart feel?' A Chinese asks, 'What will other people say?'"[1] He claimed that "the Western idea of romantic love has virtually no appeal for young adults in China."[2]

A poll of single people in India asked how many would be willing to marry someone if their potential partner had the right traits, but lacked the "emotional chemistry" of infatuation. A full 76 percent said they would get married anyway, while just 14 percent of US students said they would.* A 1988 study found that Indian "arranged" marriages rated higher in marital satisfaction than did American "love" marriages.[3] An Indian woman explained to me the experience in her culture when she said, "Love marriages start out white-hot and almost immediately cool down; arranged marriages often start out lukewarm and slowly warm up." Less than a decade into marriage (which is really just the beginning, as your first child won't even be in junior high by then) arranged marriages generally pass love marriages in intimacy and satisfaction.

I'm not advocating the *process* of arranged marriages, but I *am* suggesting that we could learn from our friends in the East about

---

* I realize I cited a similar sounding study that put the latter number at 9 percent, not 14 percent. Studies differ in their findings, but both studies demonstrate that the number is very low, whether it's 9 percent or 14 percent, or somewhere in between.

what provides a better foundation for choosing a long-term marital match. Isn't there a way we can use the wisdom applied in arranged marriages—an objective, practical look at how two people can form a family—while still accepting the reality and thrill of romantic attraction?

So, let's tie this in with the previous section: I'm not suggesting that sexual desire alone should lead you into one particular marriage, but it should lead you to take the marriage pursuit more seriously and perhaps seek a permanent relationship earlier than you might otherwise. In doing this you might have to "compromise" on feelings of infatuation, but if you can learn to give proper weight to other concerns, that's not such a big risk. Personally, I wouldn't recommend compromising on a future partner's character just so that I could become sexually active within marriage a little sooner—but if I was feeling regular temptation, I would certainly make more effort to find a suitable person to marry.

By all means, instead of staying at home and wasting time abusing pornography, watching endless romantic comedies while you complain about how no good men can be found, or passing the time on weekends looking for hookups, you're much better off putting that time and effort into finding a sole mate with whom you can seek first the kingdom of God.

WHAT ABOUT FINANCIAL STABILITY?

One of the most common arguments for delaying marriage is financial stability. As one who got married at twenty-two, I have to confess that my wife and I did indeed marry ourselves into a financial hole that took years to climb out of. On the other hand, since

I got married six years sooner than the average man does today, I also enjoyed becoming an adult with the woman I loved (not to mention seventy-two more months of guilt-free, God-honoring sex). And who's to say my wife and I wouldn't have struggled financially as singles? Between you and me, I don't see too many uber-wealthy twenty-four-year-old singles who don't have to deposit their paychecks as soon as they receive them.

On a cross-country trek with my son and his best friend, my son's friend mentioned that he was afraid getting married too young would cause him to miss out on the "single life." This guy is a committed believer—we had already talked about his desire to remain a virgin until he gets married. So I asked him, "What are you missing out on, exactly? Living with a bunch of guys, watching sports and maybe drinking beer, playing video games all weekend? Or doing that much less often but getting to spend every night with a woman you're good friends with, really attracted to, and also having an active and satisfying sexual life with?"

Listen, if you'd rather spend an evening playing Xbox with your bros and going to bed on your own than driving back to an apartment where your wife is waiting for you, well, that's up to you. But I honestly don't think you're missing out on all that much. It's a matter of personal preference, but if you're committed to living a God-honoring life—no sex before marriage, no drunkenness, not wasting gobs of time on meaningless entertainment (*some* downtime is of course appropriate), what is marriage holding you back from?

If it's about delaying marriage for a year or so to get settled in your job and gain a more solid financial footing, that's one thing. But putting off marriage to indulge adolescent fantasies of eating junk food, watching junk movies, having junk conversations, and drinking junk beer? Sorry, but I just don't see the allure.

On a positive spiritual note—I'm being vulnerable and honest here—by marrying young, I severely curtailed the possibility that my sexual drive might lead me to sin against some of God's daughters. I was able to learn how to use my body to give my wife pleasure and to meet her sexual needs instead of taking advantage of girlfriend after girlfriend as I stumbled along, only partially containing my libido. I knew I was vulnerable in that area; I don't have a perfect past. Taking stock of my spiritual weakness, early marriage seemed like a wise thing to do.

For some of you—particularly those of you who are facing the struggles I did—the call to be holy is a veiled call to get *married*. It's better to admit your weaknesses and make provision for them than to pretend you're something you're not and suffer the consequences when your true character surfaces. Caring about not hurting girls or tempting boys you've not yet dated trains you toward compassion. And compassion will serve you very well in marriage.

Being thoughtless, selfish, predatory, or sexually manipulative toward others corrupts your character. Continued failure in this area gradually turns you into a certain kind of selfish, predatory person and sets a pattern that you'll have to consciously resist and recover from later in life. This will decidedly affect the quality and climate of your marriage.

It's not just about you, not if you hope to become one-half of an intimate marriage. You're building a character, right now, by how you approach the choice to get married. And that character is the person you'll either bless or frustrate a spouse with. It's also the character you'll draw on to raise your children. Right now, today, start becoming a man or woman your kids and future spouse can respect. Make this a season of growth, not a season you'll one day wish to forget.

STUDY QUESTIONS

1. Why do you think the average age of first marriage continues to rise in our culture? Are these good reasons, consistent with Scripture, or do you think the trend should be reversed? Why?

2. How can someone who is facing tremendous sexual temptation/frustration use that as motivation to find a suitable mate to marry, while still using other criteria to choose who to marry? In other words, how can someone be motivated by sexual desire but not ruled by it when actively pursuing marriage?

3. Do you think it is wise to marry someone you highly respect and enjoy being around, but for whom you don't have intense feelings of infatuation?

4. How important is it to you to be "financially secure" before you get married? How can this be balanced against other issues?

5. Were you surprised to learn that arranged marriages often exceed "love marriages" in perceived intimacy in the second decade of marriage? How should this affect the process of choosing to get married in our culture?

9

WHAT'S YOUR STYLE?

It was a particularly sad comment, one I wish he had considered before the marriage began. A Christian athlete explained that he was divorcing his wife because, "If I wanted a model or television star, I would have married one a long time ago. All I wanted was a housewife."

There's nothing wrong with wanting to marry a woman who has an exciting career and enjoying the extra income that results—and there's nothing wrong with preferring to marry a woman who wants to focus on the home and be a full-time mom and wife. The problem is that couples often aren't honest about what they want *before* they get married, which leads to great conflict (and sadly, divorce) after marriage. When choosing someone to marry, when it comes to this issue, don't ask yourself what's "politically correct" to desire or what you *should* desire. Be honest: what do you really want? Be careful about compromising on it, because if you make an exception, you will likely regret it. Marriage is a long journey, and a small regret can grow into a great frustration that leads to divorce.

"Seeking first the kingdom of God" is a very wide umbrella. There are different ways of seeking that kingdom and expressing God's righteousness. You can be businesspeople or missionaries, you can live a life focused on the arts or athletics or media. But don't ever assume that your motivations are the same or that you even mean the same thing when you say "married." There are many different styles of marriages, but few singles ever explore this disconnect.

Here's what I want you to ask yourself as you embark on your search for a vibrant sole mate: what will your ideal marriage look like? Will the two of you spend your lives "sucking the marrow out of life," or working hard to establish a business and/or ministry (and often spending evenings and weekends recovering)? Will you seek to build a child-centered family, focusing on the kids, or have you always thought you'd like to do a lot of foreign travel or maybe just adopt one or two children? Will you have separate hobbies, or would you prefer to do everything together?

Many people assume their partner is looking for the same thing they are when they talk about "being married," but that is rarely the case. We have an image in our mind of what our marriage will be like, but we don't usually label it or even express it. We just assume that our partner shares it.

Two people who are both hungry don't necessarily want to eat at the same restaurant; two people who want to get married are not necessarily seeking the same style of relationship. In fact, many people often aren't aware of what they want. They have unspoken, unnamed assumptions. Until you see marriage patterns listed, your wants may not occur to you.

Once you become "serious" about someone to marry, you and your potential spouse need to get vulnerable and be as honest as you can be as you explore this. The temptation will be to say what you think the other person wants to hear, but that's setting up both of you for considerable disappointment and even lifelong frustration. *Lying about what you want out of marriage going in because you're afraid you'll lose the relationship if you are honest is one of the worst kinds of fraud you could ever commit.* You're asking someone to give his or her life over to a lie. And you'll eventually be found out. You can't sustain a lie for fifty years. You may worry about hurting someone's feelings if you begin to sense that the two of you aren't cut out for each other, but be more concerned about hurting that person's life. Don't serve your feelings by covering up the truth; make your feelings serve you.

To give you a practical tool to help you do this, we're going to look at some of the more common marriage "styles."[1] There are many more styles, of course, but this list will get you thinking about the possibilities. Some of these, quite frankly, are terrible reasons to get married, while others are morally neutral—a matter of preference more than values. You shouldn't get too serious with someone until you've carefully considered your own motivations and future desires and also developed a somewhat objective understanding of what your partner is looking for. The best way to be objective here is to rank yourself independently from your partner (or, for many of you, take this test before you even get a partner).

We all have a mixture of motivations, of course—I'm not trying to put any of you into a box. But I am trying to give you a tool that will help you understand your unspoken assumptions. If you allow yourself the freedom that comes from the truth that there isn't just one person you can marry, you'll be more objective and honest when going through this exercise. If your marital visions are worlds apart, marital style is not something you should compromise on.

Have you ever asked yourself, "When I say I want to get married, what *kind* of marriage am I thinking about?" Well, now you can—*after* you read this chapter.

A SPIRITUAL SOLE MATE

Let's assume the best right at the start, shall we? A spiritual sole mate is someone who is passionately committed to getting married for the glory of God first and foremost. Such people want to build a family that will model God's ministry of reconciliation to the world. They want to raise kids who will follow and serve God. They want to create a home that is a fortress for God's work on this earth. They want to partner with someone who will help them grow to become ever more like Christ.

Seeking a spiritual sole mate above all else doesn't mean you don't have *other* motivations and additional marital styles, however. There is nothing wrong, or contradictory, with wanting to marry a spiritual sole mate first but also wanting to enjoy an out-of-doors lifestyle or a companion who enjoys foreign travel. I'm hoping that the spiritual sole mate model will rule every Christian's heart, and that these other styles will be subsets, but I'm also realistic that spiritual maturity is something we grow into and that maturity brings evolving motivations. If you're already in a serious relationship, try to be honest and ask if your partner would truly pursue a "spiritual sole mate" marriage with someone else if you weren't part of the picture. In other words, does your partner really want this kind of spiritually intimate marriage, or do they just want to be married to you and know you wouldn't have it any other way? And then ask yourself, is the spiritual sole mate model of marriage something you're willing to compromise on, something you feel only mildly interested in, or something you are passionately committed to?

I can't tell you how many women have come to me with discouragement clouding their souls because they compromised on this and married spiritually anemic men. They thought everything else going well in the relationship would make up for a lack of spiritual fervor. To a woman, every one I've talked with has regretted making that compromise. If you want a spiritually rich marriage, women, you must marry a spiritually alive (and growing) man.

> Rank your desire for each of the following styles of marriage on a scale of 1 to 10 (1 = this isn't me at all, and it would be difficult for me to be married to a person who wants a marriage like this; 10 = this describes my assumed view of the marriage relationship very accurately): _____

BUSINESS BUDDIES AND ROMANTIC IDEALISTS

After Prince Charles and the future Princess Diana announced their engagement, an interviewer asked Prince Charles if the couple was "in love." Diana jumped in and answered for her future husband by saying, "Of course." Obviously flustered and taken aback, Charles added a famous addendum: "Whatever in love means." It was a painful moment, and one that proved prophetic. It seems clear, in hindsight, that Prince Charles and Lady Diana Spencer were seeking two very different things in their relationship. Charles seemed to be seeking a good match for a future king. Lady Diana's pedigree and youthful vitality seemingly fit those needs. Diana appeared to be seeking romance, fulfillment, and a storybook life.

When the marriage unraveled, Diana made it clear through various journalists that she felt betrayed (as she likely was). The earliest betrayal, however, might have been that from this early interview it was clear that the two of them were looking for two very different things in their marriage. That's a setup for major disappointment.

Some people, like Charles, are looking for a life partner who is a good "fit." Together, they can build a business, a family, a church, a name, or even rule a nation. They are not carried away by romantic notions or expectations; all that seems rather silly to them. They want a suitable partner for a satisfying and productive relationship.

Such a pragmatic matching isn't necessarily a bad thing, but if one of the partners is looking for a more romantic connection, there will be serious disillusionment when they marry someone who has a fairly utilitarian mind-set. Some guys aren't very romantic, but they feel socially inadequate and so want to marry a woman who is skilled at relationships. Some women want to find a good father for their children. Some men might have high expectations that their wife earn as much as they do.

Romantic idealists—like Diana—expect to get much of their joy and fulfillment in life from a consistently intimate marriage. They have notions that they were incomplete before they met their true love, and they expect their true love to be their best friend and constant lover, and to work hard at keeping the romance alive. They realize that infatuation will fade, but they are committed to making the relationship the center of their life (perhaps after their relationship to God).

Romantic idealists can be marked by obsessive clinginess, fear, jealousy, frequent feelings of being slighted, and even acts of desperation. I don't mean to make this sound unnecessarily negative. It's possible to be a mature and even secure person with a romantic bent; my descriptions, for the sake of clarity, travel to the extremes. Without critiquing who you think you should be, admit honestly who you are. For whatever reason, a romantic idealist's sense of security, self-worth, and happiness are directly tied with a very short leash to the current health, vibrancy, and romantic intensity of the *relationship*. This intensity is exciting and invigorating during the infatuation stage but can become exhausting afterward.

If you're a romantic idealist, you're going to become very disappointed when your partner focuses on his business or hobby. If you're married to a romantic idealist and you're not one yourself, you may become exhausted with the demands placed on you emotionally, physically, and relationally.

What are *your* expectations in this regard? What are you hoping to get out of this marriage? Do you want to join yourself to a suitable partner, or do you want to get lost in a wild, never-ending romance? (Keep in mind, if you think you're "in between," you can simply rank yourself a "5" in each category.)

Your rank:

Business Buddy: _____

Romantic Idealist: _____

ADONIS AND APHRODITE

This is a relationship based on sexual attraction and beauty. In its crassest form, it's when you see the bodybuilder marry the petite woman who has had various cosmetic enhancements. I'm not trying to suggest that every such coupling is so superficial—many times it may not be—but it helps to point out a potentially troublesome motivation. While physical attraction is a key component for marital satisfaction, if it becomes the *main* attraction, what are you going to do when your body ages?

To be fair, sometimes such attractions are due to lifestyle more than appearance. Healthy living, healthy eating, and fitness are noble values. Physical attraction as the main thing drawing the two of you together —even if it's through things like exercise and competition— is fine in your youth while you can enjoy regular exercise and joint trips to the health-food store, but what happens if your health-loving spouse gets cancer? Mutual attraction is a shaky foundation, because marriage is about growing old together more than it is about being young together. Is this a person for whom age will *increase* your devotion and respect, or will this person gradually lose what most draws you to them now? In other words, are you in this relationship largely because the sexual chemistry and attraction is so strong, or because the respect and honor you feel for this person is so deep?

If you think your partner is most drawn to you because of your beauty or strength, the relationship is in a perilous place. Beauty and strength serve a ten-year Hollywood career very well, but they're painfully short-lived servants of a fifty-year relationship.

Your rank: _____

COOKBOOK COUPLE

A "cookbook" relationship exists when one partner thinks they just need to find the right strategies, add in the correct ingredients, and then they'll get just what they want out of the relationship. You notice a cookbook relationship is forming when one partner seems somewhat obsessed with the process. ("No, we don't kiss until the third date.... We meet each other's parents at this time.... Our friends need to meet with us in this way.... You're supposed to celebrate your first Christmas/Valentine's Day/anniversary like *this*....") Such people typically read a lot of how-to books, fill out several relationship surveys, and want many sessions of relationship-oriented discussion.

I'm not suggesting that advice books aren't helpful, but if you're going to marry a cookbook spouse, you'd better be ready to participate in these kinds of discussions. They're going to want to be in marital counseling (which is a *good* thing; every couple could benefit from counseling now and then), and you can all but be assured that they will give you books and articles now and then that they will want you to read—and be very frustrated if you don't. (Do you have any idea how many women have told me they regularly check to see if the bookmark has moved in a book they've given their husbands?) And yeah, you're going to have to reserve some weekends for marriage conferences.

Again, I'm not trying to label all of these as good *or* bad descriptions; in many cases, they are a matter of preference. There can be many positive things about being married to someone who wants to improve their skills as a communicator and spouse. But some people would see such a relationship as exhausting. If a cookbook partner is marrying someone who despises that approach, there will be great frustration. If they both enjoy that sort of thing, their common bent will help them build deep intimacy rather than threaten it.

Your rank: _____

THE PASSIONATE PARTNERSHIP

A passionate partnership is marked by two people who are committed to making each other their highest priority—above recreation, child-rearing, vocation, extended family, hobbies, and just about anything else (notice I didn't say *God*). A passionate partnership can seem intimately intense and satisfying when two people enjoy it and suffocating when just one of them wants it.

A person with a passionate partnership mentality reads this and thinks, "Of course, doesn't everybody want this?"—not realizing she may be dating someone who really enjoys focusing on his business but doesn't want to talk about it when he comes home. Or a guy marries a woman who is so into her kids and homeschooling that she would perhaps rather her husband take the kids out for a nature walk when he gets home from work than spend forty-five minutes reliving his day with her. Some guys would really rather play eighteen holes of golf on Saturday morning *without* their wives. Other couples think any hobby in which both can't participate is simply unacceptable.

Of course, every marriage should prioritize the marital relationship above work and even parenting—but passionate partners take it a notch higher. They believe the relationship must be nurtured, and they are committed to keep nurturing it throughout their lives. Whatever they experience, they want to experience together, so if one is called away on a business trip, the other will try to come along.

Long conversations, plenty of time alone as a couple, and making each other the emotional center of their existence are expected, enjoyed, and cherished.

Two people sharing this vision will, indeed, maintain an intensely intimate and satisfying relationship. They will not have problems with leaving the kids for a date night or a weekend away; indeed both will be committed to this and even look forward to it. They may well look forward to becoming "empty nesters" so that they can once again focus on each other. They will not let work demands or volunteering opportunities break into their relational time together. The problem arises only when you have one who wants to have a passionate partner relationship and one who doesn't.

Your rank: _____

THE HORROR-SHOW HOUSE

This is a relationship style that has no upside, and I mention it so you can avoid it. Some people become interested in a relationship only when they are terrorized by or terrorizing their partner. It's true: the reason some people are attracted to each other is that, for reasons often related to past wounds and bent personalities, one person likes to be terrorized and one person likes to do the terrorizing.

These couples fight, argue, make each other miserable and afraid, and may even have quite vigorous makeup sex. Exhausted and spent, they peacefully coexist for another short season until routine sets in and they start the horror cycle all over again.

The problems with such a relationship are many. Often, the one who once felt comfortable being terrorized eventually gets tired of it. And this form of love is so directly in opposition to agape biblical love and marriage that it's a relationship doomed to fail.

If you feel most connected to someone when they are terrorizing you, or you feel closest to someone when you are terrorizing them, you need to know this is a spiritual sickness and a fake intimacy. You need to get healed, not married, *and in that order.* You can't build a healthy relationship on an unhealthy pattern of relating. You need to deal with this before you even think about making a lifelong choice.

I've put this in deceptively stark terms to point out its harm, but try to discern the more subtle flavors of such a matching. Does everything seem fine between the two of you—until your partner unleashes some kind of crisis? He or she gets in trouble, cheats on you, or does or says something particularly cruel? He or she apologizes, you make up and think it was a onetime event, but when things settle down and start to get routine, guess what? Another crisis erupts. This is a predictable, unhealthy pattern signifying that the two of you would rather live through terror than walk through the calm. Not only is it personally destructive, it's a prescription for parental disaster. Kids crave stability and are harmed significantly by never-ending crisis.

Your rank: _____

HOUSE AND HOME MARRIAGE

We've lived by a neighbor who was obsessed with her yard. She mowed the lawn every other day. Just about every other week, she was spreading some new fertilizer or growth aid on the grass. Every time she spoke with us, she talked about her plants, her edging, her landscaping, the health of her trees as if they were her children.

When I talked to her about a lawn-care company, she looked at me with a horrified expression: "You realize, don't you, that they will use the *same lawn mower* on your yard that they do on everyone else's? Who knows what kind of lawn disease they're spreading?"

Other people can fixate on a home's interior. If you added up how much time they spent on the Internet checking out new furniture, fixtures, home accessories, etc., it would put their Bible study to shame. Some sit in the living room, just waiting for something to break so that they can spring into action and fix it. Remodeling is, to them, a fulfilling hobby, and they will never truly be done tinkering with their house or yard.

Others see the house as a place to retreat to, but the shape, size, state, and picture-book quality have zero to do with their ego or sense of worth. They may not want to live in a messy house, and they may even enjoy living in an aesthetically pleasing house, but they certainly don't want to sacrifice Saturday or Sunday afternoons to keep up the house. They'd rather exercise, go to a movie, take a walk, or even take a nap.

This is largely a matter of choice, and when two people both enjoy dedicating themselves to their house and yard, the pairing can be quite satisfying. Where it becomes a problem is if one partner is more concerned about hospitality than house projects, or if one would rather spend two thousand dollars on a trip to Europe than on a new sofa. You're also going to run into problems if one would rather get more aggressive in their financial giving than spend the money on lawn equipment or plants.

Be honest. How will you focus your energies: on a mansion or a mission? If you're a mission person marrying a mansion person, you're going to be very frustrated. The challenge is that just about every Christian mansion person will say that they want to be a mission person. It sounds better, more spiritual. But after the wedding, they can't wait to get that new home set and will be perfectly willing to start inviting people over *after* the walls get painted, the new dining table is set up, and the hardwood floors get refinished....

Your rank: _____

THE KIDS ARE US COUPLE

Kids Are Us couples can't wait to have children—usually lots of children—and have a relationship that is often focused on the children. They may have a "date night," but even this might be done with a view toward modeling a good marriage—*for the children*. Homeschooling or expensive private schooling may often be a priority for Kids Are Us couples. This means an extra part of the budget, space in the house, or time on the clock are spent focusing on the kids. Even vacations may be chosen with educational or family fun in mind.

You can love kids, enjoy kids, and even miss parenting without being a Kids Are Us couple. But if you are truly a Kids Are Us man who marries a woman who wants, at most, two children, you will be sorely tried and deeply disappointed with your life. If you're a woman who dreams of having three natural-born children and adopting another three or four, and you're marrying a man who might, at most, be willing to put up with two of his own (biological) children, you're making a big mistake.

Your rank: _____

BOHEMIAN BUDDIES

Do you envision Sunday mornings or early afternoons taken up with reading through the *New York Times*, checking out the latest indie movie, having an apartment or house full of books, going to concerts, regular foreign travel, and fulfilling (as opposed to lucrative) vocations? That's fine, unless you marry a person who is dedicated to business, or devoted to ministry to the down-and-out, or centered around the life of the local church. This is also one of those lifestyles that usually precludes having lots of kids. It's one thing to raise ten kids on a farm or five kids in the suburbs, but it's a little more difficult to have a large family while living in Manhattan or downtown Seattle.

A lot of Christians might think of "bohemian" in negative terms (and yes, it's possible to overdo it—every couple should be involved in the local church), but the reality is, there's nothing wrong with wanting to be a redemptive presence in the arts community. However, if you truly aspire toward an arts-oriented lifestyle, you'll be frustrated hanging around with a guy or woman who puts Thomas Kinkade prints on the walls and listens to exclusively mainstream music. And this is one preference that really is difficult to compromise on. A woman can join a book discussion group if her husband doesn't read, but what about vacations? What about weekends and evenings? If he just wants to read the *Wall Street Journal* and listen to Fox News while she was hoping to check out a movie or browse a used bookstore, neither partner is going to feel much rest or intimacy on any given weekend or evening.

A quick warning here: in this section, in particular, I'm throwing around a lot of stereotypes. It's certainly possible for someone to read the *Wall Street Journal* and still be into the arts. This is intended to start a discussion, to get at the core of who you are, not to put people into boxes. The main point is to encourage you to consider who you really are rather than base your marriage on an "ideal" view of yourself that doesn't really square with reality. It's also designed to help you push past the blindness inherent in infatuation so that you can objectively evaluate whether someone you're crazy about is actually a good fit.

Even as a pastor, while I remain grateful for couples devoted primarily to their kids, or those couples whose lives seem to revolve around the local church (teaching Bible study, volunteering for VBS, etc.), and those couples whose financial success helps support the church, I also thank God for those Christians who are active participants in sometimes marginalized communities (like the arts) that often get neglected by churches because the entire community is written off as "worldly." God so loved the world that He sent His Son—isn't it at least possible that, in His Son's name, He might also send some of His children to the arts community? Do you want to be one of those people? If so, admit it, and write the number 10 in the blank below.

Your rank: _____

POLICE PARTNERS

Some people find themselves energized by a police arrangement—either they want to have somebody they can keep checking up on, or they need somebody to keep checking up on them. If one spouse is or was an addict, the other spouse will regularly check the garbage for bottles, the Internet history for sites visited, the bank statements for sudden or unexplained withdrawals.

The thing is, some people feel most comfortable fulfilling the role of a traffic cop, as it preoccupies their attention and keeps them from having to think about their own shortcomings. It gives them a sense of purpose, and sometimes even feeling fear and suspicion is more energizing than feeling bored or apathetic.

Other people like to be policed; it absolves them from having to look after themselves. They'll keep running into trouble because their partner acts like a safety net, ready to catch them so they don't hit the ground too hard. They may act like they resent the interference, but deep down, they know they need it.

The problem with entering this kind of marriage is considerable. First, if you're the policeman or policewoman, you're assuming you don't need someone to hold *you* accountable. If you're playing the criminal or save-me role, you're indulging your laziness by refusing to love, look after, or serve someone else. That makes this relationship character corrupting—reinforcing your weaknesses—rather than character forming, building up each other's strengths.

When it comes to choosing a marriage partner, avoid the messianic complex. There is only one Savior, and He hasn't been walking this earth for two millennia. Yet by accepting a partner's excuses or joining him in blaming others, some people spur on a partner who perpetually runs his life into the ground. There can be a sense of satisfaction in thinking you're the only one who really understands her, and you're the one she desperately needs, because it can feel good to be needed. There's nothing wrong with wanting to help someone out; there is something wrong with choosing an untrustworthy, crisis-prone person to become your spouse.

Before you consider such a relationship, think about something we'll touch on in more detail later on in this book: do you really want to raise kids with someone who needs to be rescued from himself or herself? If you do marry someone like that, you're almost guaranteed to become a de facto single parent. Is that truly the kind of father or mother you want to give to your children?

I recently talked with a father who said his engaged son was already "exhausted" with his fiancée's clinical mood swings. If that boy is exhausted *now*, in a dating relationship, how tired do you think he's going to be when they have three kids and he has a full-time job? You've got to think these issues through to their logical conclusion. If a relationship is wearing you down even before you're carrying a mortgage, raising children, and shouldering increased responsibilities, just try to imagine how you'll cope when other life pressures have increased as well.

Your rank_____

WARRIORS

Some people like to fight. It's what they grew up with, it's how they process emotions, it's what keeps life from being so boring. And they may even think that makeup sex is the best kind of sex.

Fighting releases adrenaline, and adrenaline can make us feel more fully alive. But it's a destructive way to stave off boredom, and it's a disastrous living arrangement in which to raise children. If you can't express what you really feel about each other without using four-letter words and hurtful comments, you lack the basic relational skills necessary to build a satisfying marriage. Either you're not ready for marriage, or the person you're with isn't capable of having an intimate marriage.

Fighting gets old. There will be seasons of life when you need encouragement, forgiveness, and acceptance; a marriage style defined by fighting usually lacks these essential qualities. Marriage is tough enough without being with someone who actually enjoys conflict. Conflict is an inevitable and necessary part of every healthy, mature relationship, but I wouldn't want to be married to someone who is energized primarily by altercations. I'd rather they be energized by service, motivated by love, and moved by compassion, kindness, and God's gentle leading. What about you?

Your rank: _____

STUDENT-TEACHER

The name explains itself. One person likes to be taught; one likes to teach. The most common form is the much older, usually financially successful man marrying a considerably younger woman (or, in the reverse form, the "cougar" relationship). He thinks it's "cute" that she is enthralled by fancy restaurants she's never been to before, and when he explains the wine list to her in a way that makes her look at him with awe, it makes him feel like a *man*.

Women can get an ego rush having a younger man chase after them, and for a while they may enjoy doing "younger" things, reliving an earlier life. But if you're talking marriage and that's the main attraction, how long can you sustain that kind of bond? Keep in mind, your "young" man won't be so young in another decade.

Due warning: "students" eventually grow up and want to be in a more mature relationship. Being a student is okay for a while, but eventually you want to graduate from school and build a life of relating. If the person you're married to won't let you do that, resentment is inevitable. You want to kill a sexual relationship? Sow the seeds of resentment. It works every time.

These are short-term situations at best and usually don't make a healthy basis for a long-term marriage.

Your rank: _____

TAKE YOUR PICK

Jennifer[2] likes to go out several times a week; she's a social butterfly and feels like Bono when he sings, "I'll go crazy if I can't go crazy tonight."[3] She's married to Riley, a guy who is into moving dirt (he develops properties for contractors) and has a propensity for working long days (ten to twelve hours is not uncommon for him once he gets the heavy machinery up and going). The hard labor makes him want to plop on the couch as soon as he gets home, and when Jennifer mentions a party or restaurant or friends getting together, Riley honestly feels that taking a shower and standing on his feet is the last thing he wants to do.

Neither Jennifer nor Riley are "right" or "wrong" in their evening preference. Working hard is just what Riley does. Needing to enjoy a good party now and then is part of Jennifer's DNA. Because Jennifer and Riley are married, they have to compromise, but in all honesty it's a constant frustration to both of them. This is something to consider *before* you get married.

Perhaps I've yet to describe your idealized marriage style. That's okay—you're not abnormal—I'm just trying to get the conversation going. Will you do yourself a favor? If you're in a serious relationship, set aside at least two, and perhaps three, "talking" dates, just the two of you, at a restaurant, a park, or anyplace you can talk without being disturbed. Beforehand, take the time to write out a description of your ideal marriage style. It might not be one that I mentioned above. Describe with *detailed* scenarios what sounds most exciting and rewarding to you.

- How will you spend your evenings?
- How close will the two of you be?
- Will you try to spend every hour outside of work together, or will you sometimes pursue separate hobbies?
- How central will church involvement be in your life?
- Will you take vacations with the kids, without the kids, or even perhaps individually?
- When you've daydreamed about the most satisfying moments of marriage, are you and your loved one walking on a beach, scouring antique stores, working on a mission field, taking your children to the park, or doing something else?

Labels aren't nearly as important as how well your assumptions about married life match up with those of the person you're thinking about marrying. How important is any one particular snapshot to you? Is it mildly interesting, very desirable, or absolutely essential? If it's the latter, and you're thinking about marrying someone who is antagonistic to that activity or style, don't try to make yourselves fit into each other's lives. We find our fulfillment in God alone; there are other people out there. Have the courage to move on and be who God made you to be. Yes, breaking up a dating relationship can be hard, even excruciating. Breaking an engagement and calling off a wedding can be even harder. No one wants to do that, especially to someone they feel deeply for. But going ahead with a wedding just because calling it off would be hurtful is one of the most foolish things a person can do. You are accepting a *life sentence* because you don't want to endure a difficult *season*.

Think about that: life sentence or difficult season. That's what you're choosing between.

After your two or three personal dates, get together with at least two other couples. Talk about marital styles. Copy this chapter and have the other couples read it first, and then get together for a group discussion. The reason this next step is so important is that sometimes guys and women are more likely to be honest when they see others sharing their views. Guys might be shy telling their girlfriend, "Yeah, I'm not so into the handyman thing," but when *another* guy says it and your guy laughs and says, "You got that right," a little moment of truth comes out. When a woman says, "You know, I don't really know if I want to have children," your girlfriend's facial expression in response will tell you a lot about what she really feels.

You might think I'm being way too obsessive about this, but trust me: this is a big deal that few couples truly consider. It's worth setting aside three or four evenings (out of your entire life, that's not much!) to make sure you're a good fit. If you're scared to do this, that means you *really* need to do it.

Remember, your goal is to build a life together. If two builders are trying to build two different houses on the same foundation, that building is going to collapse. If your dreams and your partner's dreams do not fit together, in an area that won't change, with an issue that really does matter to you, admit it. Be honest with yourself; be honest with each other. What do you envision your marriage looking like? Will you ever be able to have it with your current partner? If not, take the courageous step of ending the relationship and giving God a chance of leading you toward someone who might be a better fit. In the end, it's the most loving thing you can do.

Remember, if there's not "one right choice," there is likely a more compatible person out there with whom you can share your life in a more fruitful and satisfying manner. As painful as breaking off an engagement may be, it is nowhere near as painful as breaking up a marriage (or living in a miserable one).

STUDY QUESTIONS

1. What style of marriage best describes the kind of marriage you've always imagined having?

2. How should a couple respond if the two of them feel deeply in love but recognize that they envisage two very different styles of marriage? How important do you think agreement on marriage styles should be in deciding whom to marry?

3. What differing styles would be most compatible? Which ones would be most toxic if put together?

10

ARE YOU STRONG ENOUGH TO BE MY (WO)MAN?

Nobody who wants to keep on living wakes up one morning and suddenly decides, "I think I'll climb Mount Everest today." Such a monumental assault requires training, preparation, and gear.

Lots of gear.

In fact, experts suggest those who climb Mount Everest should approach it with no fewer than *three* separate pairs of boots: double plastic climbing boots, fully insulated overboots, and light hiking boots. And yeah—you need crampons, and certainly gaiters, and booties. Plus socks. Wool socks, pile socks, synthetic socks. Lots of socks.

Tools help keep you alive, so don't scrimp here—you'll want an ice ax, carabiners, ascenders, a rappel device, a climbing harness, trekking poles.

To stay warm, you'll need plenty of good underwear, a pile jacket, pile pants, down pants, a down parka, a Gore-Tex shell with a hood, and probably a bib. Along with your sleeping bag you'll need two different sleeping pads (and a repair kit). Plan on two pairs of synthetic gloves and two pairs of pile mitts or Gore-Tex overmitts. Hand warmers are optional, but you won't regret bringing them.

For your head you'll want a baseball cap or some kind of sun hat, at least a visor. At other times you'll want a ski hat that covers your ears. Get a heavy and a light balaclava. Many climbers also like to use a neoprene face mask, and make sure you include a headlamp (with plenty of extra bulbs and batteries).

You're still not done, though. Sun on snow equals a blinding headache, so take two pairs of glacier sunglasses, and don't even think about anything less than 100 percent UV protection. Also, ski goggles to go over the glasses.

And toilet paper. *Please* don't forget the toilet paper.

Climbing Everest is a big deal. You need to be prepared. The same is true for marriage. Just as you wouldn't try to scale a mountain without making sure you have what you need, don't enter the most difficult relationship of your life without doing so. Life is not going to be easy. Prepare for it to be really hard—twice as hard as you think it's going to be. If it ends up being less difficult than you thought, there's nothing lost having married someone who could have weathered the storm with you. If you plan on it being a picnic and marry someone who is only good for the easy times, then you're going to be in serious trouble when times turn tough.

I don't want to sound callous, but if a buddy of mine who weighed 325 pounds and couldn't walk a lap around the track without having to stop for a rest offered to accompany me on a trek up Everest, I'd decline. I'd have to say, "Hey, I love you, and I'll watch a movie with you or take a walk around the park with you, but I'm not climbing Everest with you."

Some people may *want* to be married to you, but they may not have what it takes. When you're dating and in love, it's not that difficult to build and enjoy a relationship. It doesn't take someone of great character to accompany you to movies and nice restaurants, to go on fun bike rides or hikes or sit in a Starbucks or make out on a couch. Most people can do that.

That's not real life, however—at least, not for very long. As a pastor, I've had to watch couples endure some excruciating life crises. Is the person you're thinking about marrying capable of facing crises like the following?

MEDICAL MAELSTROMS

Ever hear of Angelman syndrome? I've met three families who have given birth to children with this neurogenetic disorder marked by severe intellectual and developmental delays. Google it; watch some videos on YouTube. There is no cure for this malady, meaning today's parents will have to take care of such a child for the rest of their lives.

Just last night I had dinner with a man whose daughter began showing the effects of autism by the time she turned two. They love their daughter; God is doing great things in her life and in their lives. But if this man had married a superficial woman who was embarrassed by her girl's lack of social interaction instead of moved to compassion, the story would be very different. A shockingly high percentage of marriages with severely disabled children end in divorce, because it's not easy. There's a temptation to expend so much time, energy, and money caring for a disabled child that some unwise parents allow their marriage to exist on leftovers. Being physically exhausted, experiencing spiritual confusion (when God doesn't answer your prayers the way you want Him to), dealing with interrupted sleep schedules, having to give up hobbies or drive older cars to pay for extra medical care—how would the person you're thinking about marrying hold up under this kind of stress?

They just might have to.

Darell had to wear a big tux when he got married, not because he was fat but because he was a bodybuilder who could bench-press four hundred pounds. You don't fit pecs like that into a 38R coat. His wife, Stacey, married a physically fit man, the kind of man in whose arms she could feel both lost and safe, covered and protected.

Just twenty-four months into their marriage, however, Darell started experiencing some disconcerting symptoms—numbness, vision issues, tremors. After some tests, the news came as a shock: Darell had multiple sclerosis. He fought off going into a scooter for as long as possible, but his legs couldn't carry him fully much past his forty-fifth birthday. Friends, that leaves a lot of life, a lot of marriage, to be lived. For most of their days together, even though Stacey married a strong, bodybuilding husband, she's had to carry in the groceries and do most of the heavy lifting.

Jake married an accomplished businesswoman, Grace, who worked for a prestigious consulting firm. She had the kind of job that sets you up vocationally for life. If you wanted to get an MBA, they'd get you into Harvard or Wharton. If you wanted to work for a nonprofit or another company, they'd help you do that, too. If you wanted to stay with them and slowly grow rich, well, by all means, pull up a seat, get to work, and prepare to cash the checks.

For a couple of years Grace earned more money than Jake did, until an autoimmune disorder began to take over her body and eventually left her bedridden for more than six months. The company was generous—for a while. Eventually, Jake and his wife and the company realized Grace wasn't coming back. Jake thought he was marrying a woman who would more than double his income (but that wasn't why he married her, of course); now he's married to a woman who will need him to support her, perhaps for the rest of her life.

You don't know what the future holds, but you *can* know the kind of character you're marrying. The spiritual capacity to hope, even in the face of seemingly insurmountable obstacles, is an essential quality in life—"Against all hope, Abraham in hope believed" (Rom. 4:18). Don't minimize the importance of marrying someone who is spiritually tough, who doesn't grumble and forget all about God at the first sign of trouble. Life is usually full of trouble.

If you marry for money, health, or looks, keep in mind that none of these are certain to remain. Character is the surest thing. Even if the two of you manage to avoid a medical maelstrom, the vast majority of you will have to navigate something else that will test you to your core: having children. Does the person you're planning on marrying have what it takes in this regard? Are they strong enough not just to be your spouse, but to be your children's mom or dad?

YOUR KIDS' PARENT

During an interview, a Hollywood actress didn't rave to a reporter about her husband's wealth, looks, or reputation. Instead, watching her husband on set with one of their children, she said, "The one thing I can say I did a good job on, I found a great man to father kids with. It's like if I didn't do anything else right in this world, my kids got a good doggone daddy."[1]

Right now, your children are theoretical. When they take on actual flesh and blood, you will experience emotions and a capacity for sacrificial love that you never even knew existed. You would be willing to swim across the ocean in a lead coat in order to save them. The most significant act of love, however, takes place before they're born. Before you agree to marry anyone, ask yourself, "Is this the best mother/father I can find for my children?" The time will come when, like this actress, you will be more grateful than you can imagine, or more regretful than you've ever been, because you have chosen for them a wonderful or below-average parent.

For starters, what you'll want more than anything else is for those babies to be with you for all eternity. You're going to want them to become Christians. It won't feel like "want." It'll feel like "need."

One mother approached me and asked me to speak with her daughter, a young woman who claimed to be a "seriously committed" Christian who was planning on marrying a young man who declared himself an agnostic and whose parents were Buddhists. I got right to the point.

"Do you want your future children to become Christians?"

"More than anything," the young woman replied.

"Then let me paint you a scenario. Your husband never goes with you to church, but you take your boy every week. When that boy turns eight, he asks his dad, 'Dad, why don't you come to church with us?' and Dad answers, 'Son, I don't believe that stuff. I think that stuff is for women, mostly.'"

Pausing for full effect, I asked her, "Who do you think that eight-year-old boy is going to feel pulled toward? Do you think hearing a dad he idolizes talk down faith is something that will help him grow toward God or get in the way? And then when he spends the night at Grandpa and Grandma's house, and sees their Buddhist shrine, and hears them talk about their faith, you've got a little kid who sees one parent go to a Christian church, one parent talk down faith altogether, and grandparents who practice an entirely different religion. I don't see how, if you want your future kids to become Christians 'more than anything else,' this is the kind of marriage you'd consider."

In addition to wanting your kids to know the one true God, you're also going to want them to be loved by *both* parents. Not tolerated, not merely provided for, but engaged with, loved, cherished. Watching your spouse love on and play with your kids will move you like few other things ever will. There may come a day when you have a terrible argument with your spouse, but then, later in the day, you watch him or her do something marvelous for one of your kids, and your heart will immediately melt with affection.

You're not just choosing a life partner. You're choosing your kids' future mom. You're choosing your kids' future dad. Is this person worthy of that job? Does he or she have what it takes?

Women, if you don't want your boys to grow up to be just like the guy you're marrying, you're looking at the wrong man. Men, if you couldn't tell your sons, "Find someone exactly like your mom to marry," then she's not the one for you. Your boyfriend or girlfriend isn't just applying to be your spouse; the job is much, much bigger than that. Make sure they're capable of being an outstanding parent. Ask your friends; ask your family members. Get some objective observations.

Sometimes singles contemplating marriage *do* think about the kind of parent they're choosing. It's very rare, however, that they consider the impact of grandparents, but you should. Do your loved one's parents have what it takes to play a significant role in your future children's lives?

YOUR KIDS' GRANDPARENTS

This one is a little tougher and not quite as absolute as the previous category, but it's still something to consider: you're not just choosing your kids' future parent, you're choosing your kids' future grandparents. If you want to build a family of faith, it's helpful to have a legacy to build on. It's a huge assist to have another couple who will actively pray for your child and who will speak and act in such a way that affirms what you're trying to do at home (this is *especially* the case if your own parents are whacked-out). Your kids will see their grandparents share your faith, treat each other a certain way, and talk about others a certain way. That creates a stability and gives them that much more of a foundation from which their own faith can be conceived and nurtured.

In his book *Stepping Up*, Dennis Rainey tells the tear-drenched story of how his daughter Rebecca and her husband, Jake, gave birth to a little baby whose brain was almost gone by the time she was born. Little Molly lived just seven days, but in that one love-packed week, she received abundant care, prayers, and comfort. Because both Rebecca and Jake come from strong families, *two* sets of grand-parents were there, praying over little Molly, reading Scripture to her, and singing songs of worship along with her parents. Here's how Dennis describes Molly's final moments on earth, when they all knew she was about to die and planned their last good-byes:

> Barbara was first. It was quite a maneuver to make sure all the wires and tubes that were supporting Molly's life didn't get tangled, but finally there she was in her arms. Barbara kept saying how much of an honor it was to hold this little princess of the King. She held her close and cooed words of love and admiration over her beautiful face. Holding back tears was impossible.
>
> When it was Bill's turn, he stroked her face, tenderly whispered his love for her, and shared his favorite scriptures with her. Pam beamed as she gently rocked Molly and sang "Jesus Loves Me" to her. Both Bill and Pam just held her, kissing her face, holding her little hands, and weeping as they said good-bye.
>
> As Molly was placed in my arms, she felt so warm, just like every newborn. I tried to sing to her, and I doubt that she recognized "Jesus Loves Me" as I choked out a few words through tears.[2]

As his own kids were growing up, Dennis used to tell stories of a fantasyland filled with "Speck people." Dennis always got one of the Speck people into a harrowing dilemma and then said, "And you'll have to wait until tomorrow night to hear the rest of the story." He now frequently told these stories to his grandchildren, so Jake asked his father-in-law, Molly's grandfather, to tell her one Speck story before she died.

At first, Dennis protested—he just couldn't. But Jake and Rebecca implored him, which led to this:

> I held little Molly, looked into her face, and began my story: "A Speck grandfather and his Speck granddaughter went fishing for tiny Speck fish...." My story was less than sixty seconds long, and when I looked up into Rebecca's face, she had the biggest grin, dimples and all. She was loving the moment.
>
> As I concluded my story, I told Molly, "The Speck grandfather and granddaughter took their fish and ate them, and then they encountered something you would never expect or believe ... and you will have to wait until I get to heaven to hear the rest of the story."
>
> At this point I was sobbing, but I got the words out ... and Rebecca and Jake started laughing. Rebecca's laughter has always been contagious, and I, too, began to really laugh.[3]

Losing a child is one of the most painful experiences any human can ever know. But the corporate love of four faith-filled grandparents allowed this young mom and dad to actually find *laughter* and *hope* in the face of one of life's ugliest realities.

It gets even better: with all the laughter in the room, little Molly's oxygen monitor, which had been at an anemic 80 percent, shot up to 92 percent, then 94, 97, 98, 99, and then, finally, 100. That tiny newborn drank in the faith and hope and laughter of her parents and grandparents. Though this was ultimately her last day on earth, I don't doubt that she died knowing she was very loved, and she is no doubt eagerly waiting in heaven to greet first her grandparents, and then her parents, who gave her such a sweet and blessed passing.

You have a chance—one opportunity—to choose such a legacy for yourself and for your children.

That's the positive view. On the negative end, if there are dangerous issues in your boyfriend's or girlfriend's prior generations, be very cautious. Child abuse, sexual deviancy, psychological problems, and addictions not only will make your potential spouse more vulnerable as he or she ages (some of these problems take a while—until a person is in his or her midthirties—to sprout) but can also be passed down, in some sense, to your kids. I'm not saying it's always direct, but the statistical evidence is pretty frightening.

A Facebook friend who has been through three divorces sent this message to me: "What I didn't know when I met or married this guy [husband number three] was that there was a family history of mental illness. You just don't think to ask, 'So, has anyone in your family ever had a lobotomy?? Really?? Two of your uncles?? And one nearly killed his wife and kids?? Really??' There are mentally ill people, male and female, who are capable of becoming/saying/doing anything they think will help them accomplish a goal. This guy I married was physically and sexually abusive…. He was a Jekyll/Hyde, a liar/ deceiver, and I didn't recognize the wolf in sheep's clothing."

My friend had already been through *two* divorces. You might think she would be extra cautious about husband number three. But the heart, when it's engaged, can shut down the mind and resist any sense of caution. She would be the first to tell you to thoroughly do your homework in checking out those delicate issues buried in a potential spouse's family history.

Never forget: *you're building a family.* To make a wise investment, you need to consider the other "partners." Is your spouse so strong in every other area that you're willing to take a risk here even if he or she has a weak extended family? Or does your potential spouse barely qualify on his or her own *and* have a nightmare extended family as well? If the latter is the case, you might try to do a little better.

For those of you considering remarriage, and especially those of you who have kids, if your potential spouse keeps telling you what a nut job their ex-spouse is, ask yourself as a parent, "Do I want to bring my kids into that kind of situation?"

This might sound harsh, but look at it this way. If three people applied to babysit my kids, the mere fact that they all wanted a job wouldn't be what I based my choice on. I'd hire the babysitter who seemed most stable, safe, qualified, and competent. That's not being selfish or judgmental; it's being wise, responsible, and protective of my kids.

You get to start protecting your kids before they're even born. Give them a godly mom or dad. Even better, raise them in a godly family with lots of spiritual support. Most young people completely discount this. I think it should be much more of a factor in your final decision than many people make it.

A HUMBLE SPIRITUALITY

If the person you love knows you're a Christian and says he or she's a Christian too, that means almost nothing. In one sense, it means a lot, in that if they categorically say they're not a believer, you have no business marrying them. However, I hope you want more than just someone who simply *says* he or she's a Christian. Consider marrying a certain kind of Christian, one with a humble spirituality.

Does your Christian pray? Not just in church and not just with you, but on his or her own? If not, you'll walk through life without the person who knows you most lifting you up in prayerful support. You'll be the only one supporting your kids in prayer. You'll be married to someone who isn't opening themselves up to God's conviction, encouragement, and support. If your spouse gets depressed, you'll have to lift that person up on your own, since he or she won't know how to go to God. If you get depressed, you'll have to find another friend to prayerfully support you because your spouse won't know how to. If your husband or wife develops bad attitudes toward you or cultivates sinful habits, and isn't spending time in prayer to be convicted by God, those attitudes and habits will grow stronger and possibly threaten your marriage.

Is your potential future spouse a student of the Bible? Humble Christians know they have a lot to learn. If you marry a man or woman who opens his or her Bible only when the pastor is reading the text, you're marrying someone whose spiritual growth will be negligible. That person won't be growing in wisdom. She won't have

Scripture on her mind to encourage you or spiritually feed your children. He'll be set in his own prejudices and faulty thinking without being washed by the Word. A spouse like this will never be spiritually wiser than he or she already is.

Finally, by "humble" spirituality I mean, does your Christian understand he or she is not perfect and needs to grow? Does that person resent it when you notice his or her anger, lust, selfishness, or does he or she recognize that while God is working on them, there is always room for more growth? If people don't understand God's grace, they will get defensive rather than listen. If they don't understand God's grace, they will never be empowered to rise above an ineffective perfectionism that leads to legalism and denial. You will be married to someone who spends all of his or her energy covering up and making excuses instead of repenting and changing. Worse, you'll be married to someone who doesn't even think he or she needs to change (which means, by extension, that your spouse will think you're the one who is always in the wrong).

Let me say a word to the women here: at least 90 percent of the change in my marriage has come through God convicting me in prayer and Bible study. Less than 10 percent has come about from my wife confronting me or talking to me. I study marriage *for a living*. I've written over half a dozen marriage-related books (some with others) and speak on marriage twenty weekends a year. I try really hard to understand marriage and to serve my wife. But if God wasn't an active force in my life, a *daily* presence, I'd fear for my wife's security, happiness, and even sanity. I'd drive her crazy with my selfishness, weakness, sin, and pride. Though I have miles of improvement ahead of me, God is continually making me into a much better husband than I'd be otherwise. *God* is doing this, not me. Can I suggest that this is something you want in your husband as well? He might be a great guy, but for my daughters I'd take an average guy who is growing in God over a great guy who is spiritually stagnant any day, because it's only a matter of time until that average guy starts treating his wife like gold and the great guy becomes a little less so. It's one thing for selfishness to mark a twenty-five-year-old husband; it's particularly sad when a fifty-year-old husband shows the same trait.

So, to sum it all up: the man or woman you're thinking of marrying should be someone whose character can survive major life challenges. Your potential future spouse should be the best parent you can find for your kids and ideally bring along some spiritually beneficial grandparents as well. And he or she should be steeped in a humble spirituality, a deep desire to drink from God's well and grow in Christ throughout the rest of his or her life.

Before you breathe a sigh of relief, however, realize that we're just getting started. We've mentioned some character issues in this chapter; in the next, we're going to talk about some necessary *skills*. Someone could be "strong enough" to be your man or woman but still lack the competence and capability of being an excellent husband or wife.

STUDY QUESTIONS

1. How difficult do you expect marriage to be? On a scale of 1 to 10 (1 = always easy, if you're truly in love; 10 = a difficult challenge every day) what do you expect to face?
2. How do you think a person's perception of the difficulty of marriage will influence *who* they marry?

3. Would you consider marrying someone you felt deeply in love with, even if you don't think they're very mature or if they lack basic relational skills? Where do you draw the line—how mature must someone be (relationally) in order for you to feel comfortable marrying them?

4. Have you known any families or couples that had to endure serious medical difficulties? From what you've observed, what did that do to their relationship? How might what you observed affect the qualities of the person you're looking for to marry?

5. Would you be willing to marry someone who makes you laugh, who you enjoy being around, and who you are sexually attracted to, even if you're not sure they'd be a good parent? Why or why not?

6. How can you tell ahead of time how good a parent someone might be?

7. Describe the ideal grandparents for your future children. How important does giving your children grandparents like this seem to you?

11

MAKING A MARRIAGE

Most Hollywood romances focus on finding "the one." A common plot point, early in the movie, is to have two individuals, destined to be together, almost meet. They'll walk right past each other, perhaps even glance and smile as they pass, enter and exit the same room, bus, or café just seconds apart, or they'll be on opposite sides of the same park as the camera hovers overhead. If only she would walk *that* way, she'd run into him; if only he had turned his head one second sooner …

Since the actors are the two best-looking people on the set, you know they will meet eventually, but it creates a little tension to put it off for a while.

This romantic mind-set is based on the false and harmful notion that a good relationship is something you find, when in fact it is something you make. Infatuation is something you find. Sexual chemistry is something you find. A lost cell phone is something you find. But a strong, intimate, God-honoring marriage that leads to a lifelong partnership and that fosters a sense of oneness? That's something you *make*, and it takes a long time to make.

I want to say this again, because if you'll accept this premise, it'll go a long way toward helping you make a wise marital choice: a good marriage isn't something you find, it's something you make.

A relationship, by its very definition, can't be found; it has to be built. It requires two people getting to know each other, and then every day they have to choose to keep relating to each other or risk drifting apart. Intimacy is created stitch by stitch, through verbal sharing, dedicated praying, acts of love and service, expressions of commitment, and building increased understanding through regular communication and by experiencing life together.

In fact, one study suggests that it takes from nine to fourteen years—at least a decade, and sometimes a decade and a half—for two individuals to stop thinking of themselves as individuals and to start thinking of themselves as a couple. That's right—the journey from "me" to "we" takes years to achieve. That's due in part to the way our brains are wired. In a very real sense, we shape our brains with our lifestyle; the things we do and the habits we choose create neural pathways that become our new norm. That's how addictions are built; that's why habits can be so difficult to break.

Put it this way: have you ever driven home from work or church, pulled into your driveway, and realized you didn't make a single conscious decision the entire drive home? That you were essentially on autopilot? That's neuroplasticity in action. Your brain has become so familiar with that route that once you start out on it, habit takes over. You almost stop seeing the journey as individual turns and instead process it as one basic decision: go home.

Relationally, if you've been living as a single for twenty to thirty years and then get married, your brain doesn't immediately turn into "Okay, I'm married now; I have to think like a married brain, act like a married brain, stop putting up the defenses of a single brain, and embrace the intimacy of a married brain." Those patterns of relating that served you as a single must be dismantled. You have to consciously adopt new forms of thinking and learn how to understand, serve, forgive, be vulnerable, move toward someone rather than away even in the face of hurt, and drop your former defenses. You are no longer evaluating this person; you are dedicated to sacrificially loving them. It takes time for you to make such a monumental cognitive shift. To reach true intimacy and that sense of oneness that we all desire requires two things: the initial death of infatuation (which doesn't recognize reality and therefore can't serve true intimacy) and at least nine to ten years of practice, faithfully moving toward each other relationally.

Neurologically, a relationship can be built, and it can be systematically torn apart or die of neglect, but it is not "found" or "lost."

With this being true, when it comes to choosing someone to marry, it is imperative that you choose someone who is both capable and willing to "climb Mount Everest," to make a marriage with you. I stress the word *both* because while some might be *willing*, they may not be capable. Others might be capable but not willing. You want to find someone who can and will do both. If not, they are the wrong person for you.

HOW TO MAKE THE MARRIAGE

The following characteristics are essential to make a marriage. You can't expect a twenty-two-year-old to possess all of them in their full mature form, but you should see the foundations of these elements. The degree to which they are not present is the degree to which you'll have difficulty building intimacy with this person and the degree to which you're going to struggle in the early years of marriage.

IS HUMBLE

A quick definition: humility is not thinking less *of* yourself, it is thinking less *about* yourself. It is someone who, like Jesus, believes he has come "not to be served, but to serve." Jesus knew His talents, and He knew His deity, but He used His power to serve. Unlike Jesus (since we are not perfect, and He was), a humble person is someone who has experienced and is experiencing conviction of sin: they are aware that they fall short, every day, and that they have much to work on, and biblical grace is the only place they put their hope.

The only thing worse than marrying an imperfect person is marrying an imperfect person who thinks he or she is perfect. When you lovingly confront them, they'll take offense. Or, horrified that they've been found out, they'll minimize the issue with silly games: "I'm just a horrible, horrible wife." No, you're a good wife who has a sinful issue that needs attention. The reason I call this a "game" is that unparticular repentance is a clever way to avoid particular conviction. Saying "everything about me is rotten" helps us sidestep the fact that some parts of us are more rotten than others.

While theologically it is true that "all our righteous acts are filthy rags," that doesn't mean we don't have some strengths and weaknesses. A wise person knows he might excel at giving but lack patience, or excel in patience while lacking courage. The key is to accept that there will always be weaknesses in our lives and, with a spirit of willingness and appreciation, to learn to value a spouse who wants to help us make every effort to add to our faith (2 Pet. 1:5–7).

Humility matters more than money and appearance, as it is the character foundation of growth and godliness. You can always earn more money, lose a little weight, and gain a bit more muscle, but if someone's character has no foundation, there's nothing to build on. Humility is the cornerstone of character and the foundation of a growing, intimate relationship. I don't believe it is possible for a highly arrogant person to be intimately connected with someone. Arrogant people use people; they don't love them. Besides, the Bible says no less than three times: "God opposes the proud but gives grace to the humble." Do you want to marry someone who is at war with God, or someone who is walking in His grace?

A humble person:

- Lives with biblical conviction of our overall sin nature as well as particular sins.
- Lives out of the gospel—that we are helpless to save or even change ourselves, apart from the work of Christ and the empowerment of the Holy Spirit.
- Is open to receiving appropriate correction and eager to take action when faults are pointed out.
- Lives authentically—is concerned with growing in righteousness rather than merely appearing righteous.
- Aspires to excel in being a servant.

When she gets into an argument, a humble person considers the fact that she may be wrong and that there may be something she has missed or is overlooking. She is more concerned with walking in light and truth than with being right. Aware of his spiritual poverty, a humble person prays and studies and confesses and asks people to hold him accountable, as he knows he is a work in progress.

IS ABLE TO FORGIVE

If you believe the Bible, you are going to stumble many times throughout your marriage (James 3:2). You will break your spouse's heart. You will disappoint her. You will embarrass him. Your sin will inconvenience her.

A couple I was pastorally counseling needed to work on building some relational intimacy. The guy confessed that he didn't want to fully open up to his fiancée about the stress in his life because he didn't want to be a burden to her. I told him that if his goal is to never be a burden to his future wife, he shouldn't marry her; he might as well break up with her right now. There was, quite understandably, visible shock on his face until I explained, "What if you get laid off and can't find another job and she has to double her hours? What if you get a stroke and she has to hand-feed you? What if you make a really stupid investment or a dumb mistake and get fired or have your portfolio tank? One or all of those things will happen over the course of your marriage. You are going to hurt and disappoint this woman very deeply, so you might as well learn how to do it productively."

It's hard to accept that we are going to hurt someone we love so much, but if we marry them, we will. *That's a biblical promise.* Which means forgiveness is absolutely essential. I have seen married couples survive affairs, catastrophic illnesses, financial meltdowns, and tragedies that would make you pass out—but the one thing I have never seen a marriage survive is a persistent unwillingness to forgive.

How do you know the person you love is capable of forgiving? First, that person recognizes his or her own need for forgiveness, understands God's love and acceptance, and not only believes the gospel but has it woven into every fiber of his or her being: we are all sinners saved by grace who depend on God's mercy and initiating grace every hour of our lives.

Can I be honest with you? If your boyfriend or girlfriend is having a difficult time forgiving you for things you've done while dating, marriage is going to be even harder. When you live together and raise a family together, sins become more apparent, more common, and more consequential. If that person can't forgive you *now*, he or she will never be able to forgive you *then*.

Forgiveness does not mean the removal of consequences, of course. Women, if your guy cheats on you, you need to forgive him—and most likely, break up with him. If he hits you, even once—you will have to work toward forgiveness, but I pray you will end the dating relationship right there (more on this in a moment) and perhaps even turn him in to the police.

In addressing forgiveness, I'm talking about the kinds of sins that don't speak of a questionable character but rather of a person in progress who needs common grace. Dating is different from marriage—it is appropriate to evaluate your commitment and the person's worthiness, as their character reveals itself. Once you are married, you have to look at these things differently, but until you are married, evaluation is essential.

HANDLES CONFLICT IN A HEALTHY WAY

Because both of you stumble in many ways, you need someone who can not only forgive but can work through conflict in a healthy way. *There will be conflict.* The only question is, will you grow toward each other as a result of the conflict, or will your hearts grow ever colder because you avoid the issue or because you respond to conflict in hurtful ways?

Unhealthy conflict resolution includes the silent treatment or stonewalling—a pathetic, passive-aggressive refusal to act like a person in a relationship. Also unhealthy is any form of violence—threats, yelling, and any physical violence.

Women, I'm pretty legalistic on this one, but let me lay this out: when it comes to physical abuse in dating, my suggested rule is, one strike and he's out. He doesn't get a second chance. If he's a little too angry for you when you're dating, he will become much too angry when you're married. A man who expresses anger with physical violence is on a pathway toward family destruction. Do you really want to make babies with a guy who will get angry at them and then hit them? Do you want to sleep naked next to a man who might do you bodily harm? Do you want to take showers in a house when he could walk in at any moment and hurt you when you are in a completely defenseless state? Do you want to argue with a man in a kitchen and worry about the fact that there is a block of knives two feet away from where he's yelling at you? Do you want to drive in an SUV with a guy who can't control his temper and may run both of you into a head-on accident (while your children are riding in the backseat)?

Some may accuse me of being too unyielding on this, but I believe that if a boyfriend hits you, that's all you need to know. He's not right for you. That's not the kind of guy you want to marry. Many, many women have ignored evidence of "a little" violence in their boyfriend and have lived to regret it. That's why I think that if there's *any* violence, you end the relationship right there (and of course, this goes for men dating violent women as well). Assume he's on his best behavior while trying to win you over. If he can't keep things under control while you're dating, he'll never be able to handle himself being around you every day. Don't do this to yourself, don't do this to your future children, don't do this *to him*!

The best thing that could happen for an abuser would be for him to lose someone he really loves due to his acting out. That might force him to seek help and to learn healthier ways of relating. If you make an "exception" just this once, you are training him to expect women "who really love him" to give him a hall pass when it comes to violence. He needs to learn that physical violence is a completely unacceptable way of solving conflict with a woman, particularly with his wife.

If your husband's strength threatens you instead of comforts you, you will never have a life of true intimacy with him. Don't marry that guy.

A woman once told me I'm too black-and-white on this, but before you agree with her, consider this: if out of romantic silliness you ignore signs of a man's violence, you may one day have to tell your kids, "I'm sorry that I chose a dad for you who scares you. I'm sorry you've seen your mother threatened, maybe even hit. I'm sorry we all feel a little bit safer when your dad is gone, and a little nervous whenever he comes home. However, the infatuation I felt for him was so strong, I think, all in all, it's been worth it."

Another form of unhealthy conflict resolution is to talk *about* your partner before you talk *to* your partner. There is nothing wrong with seeking godly input in appropriate fashion. There is something wrong with complaining about your partner to your friends or family members in a nonredemptive way. That's called gossip. If you haven't talked about it to your partner, you have no business talking about it to someone else, unless it's a particularly touchy issue and you're seeking godly wisdom as to how to share it or broach the topic. Talking about conflict with others should never be a substitute for talking with your spouse; it merely prepares you to talk to your spouse.

Healthy conflict resolution, on the other hand, means a person can admit where he or she is wrong. Even if someone is only 10 percent wrong, that person can own the 10 percent. But it is *not* healthy to confess wrongdoing when there is no wrongdoing to confess. Some people will say "sorry" when there is nothing to be sorry for, just to bring about peace. That's not healthy, and it's not biblical. You want to find someone humble enough to admit personal failings, wise enough to recognize yours, and courageous enough to hold his or her ground if you are acting arrogantly and refusing to see your sin.

Finally, people who resolve conflict in a healthy way will be willing to seek a third opinion in the face of stalemate. There will be times in your marriage when the two of you cannot come to complete agreement, and you may need to find a godly pastor or counselor to hear both of you out and provide wise counsel. I would be hesitant to marry anyone who wouldn't agree, going in, to use counseling when necessary, for the simple fact that it *will* be necessary. I wouldn't marry a woman who was afraid to visit the doctor, because I know her body will eventually get sick and need medical attention. Likewise, I wouldn't marry a woman who was afraid to seek a relational doctor, because I know there will be moments when our marriage will get sick and need outside attention.

Entering a new marriage is like buying a new car: it runs fine for a while. But eventually that shiny new car is going to need a mechanic. If you're marrying someone who resents mechanics or who is afraid of mechanics or who is threatened by mechanics, you'd better get used to walking, because your car is going to be broken for a really long time.

COMMUNICATES

Intimacy is built through sharing, listening, understanding, and talking through issues. If someone doesn't like to talk, refuses to talk, or resents your desire to talk, intimacy building is going to hit a stone wall. In most relationships, the woman will desire to talk more than the man, so women shouldn't freak out if their boyfriends don't seem as excited about this aspect of relational building as they are. But, women, if he isn't growing in his desire to share his heart with you, if he is doing it only to please you, if it feels like a chore to him to get to know you, if he can't or won't ask you a question about yourself—he lacks the basic relational skills to build an intimate marriage.

The general rule is this: however much your boyfriend talks to you while dating, cut that down by at least 25 percent after marriage. If you're not good with that, you're looking at the wrong guy. I'm not saying it should be that way, only that it almost always is.

Talk to married women; ask them if this isn't true. Make your choice accordingly.

PRAYS

Why would anyone want to be married without having God as a partner? I can't imagine facing the challenges of marriage without the hope of God to lift my eyes when I'm discouraged and the conviction of God to open my eyes when I'm blind to my own sin. Since marriage is something you make, and since marriage is going to be difficult, I'd want to marry someone who knows how to pray, who practices prayer, and who is growing in prayer.

A woman once told my wife and me that she feels so much safer when she knows her husband is praying and in the Word. She doesn't have to ask him if he's doing this—she can tell by his attitude, his actions, the tone of his voice, his overall demeanor. And knowing that he is regularly connecting with God gives her a peace and security that she treasures.

MAKES AND KEEPS FRIENDS

Does your future spouse have friends? Not acquaintances, but true friends? If someone is twenty-eight years old and doesn't really have many or even any close connections, that's a signal that person may not be very skilled at building intimate friendships. What makes you think it will be any different with you? At the very least, you need to know you will have to do much of the work to turn this marriage into a friendship, and you're assuming your boyfriend or girlfriend is going to be willing and/or capable of responding in an intimate way. It's always dangerous to assume someone can or will change. Your best bet to make a marriage is to find someone who already knows how to make and keep friends.

MAKE THE CALL

Okay, now you know some of the basic requirements to build a marriage. If you're in a relationship that appears headed toward marriage, here's a simple test. On a separate piece of paper, rank your potential spouse on a scale of 1 to 10 in each area. This person:

is humble. _____
is forgiving. _____
resolves conflict in a healthy way. _____
knows how to communicate. _____
prays. _____
is skilled in the art of friendship. _____

If your total score isn't a forty-five or higher, I think you need to talk this list through with a pastor, trusted older friend, or counselor to see if the person you're thinking about marrying is going to be capable of building the kind of marriage you desire. If the person you are thinking about marrying lacks the basic skills required to make a marriage, the death of infatuation is going to hit you particularly hard. You won't have a partner who can respond to this necessary life moment by slowly building relational intimacy on a day-by-day basis. You know what that means? Let me put it bluntly: get ready to live a lonely life. You will be able to cope for a while, by sharing the task of raising children together and then by pursuing same-gender friendships so you have someone to talk to now and then. But know this: eventually those children will grow up and leave the house. Some of those friends will move away. And you're going to be facing another thirty years of marriage to a person who isn't capable of relating to you on a meaningful level.

It all comes down to this: if relational intimacy matters to you, make sure you marry someone who has the basic skills to build such a relationship, as well as the motivation to keep on doing so. Once the infatuation ends, relational skills are essential to take your marriage to the next level. This sounds rather elementary, but it's often ignored in the fog of infatuation.

STUDY QUESTIONS

1. Had you ever thought of this before: "A good marriage isn't something you find; it's something you make"? Do you think it's true? Why or why not?
2. People often consider whether they feel attracted to each other physically, while ignoring things like the person's level of humility. How would you balance your value of a person's physical attractiveness with their level of spiritual humility?
3. Have you ever asked someone to forgive you? What was that experience like? Was that reaction something similar to what you hope to experience in marriage or something very different?
4. Does conflict scare you? What characteristics should a future mate have in order for a couple to grow through conflict, instead of being crushed by it?
5. Do you agree that any serious act of violence should end a dating relationship? Why or why not? What constitutes "serious" in your mind?

6. How important do you think regular communication will be for you to fully enjoy your marriage and feel connected to your spouse? How can you tell if someone will communicate after the infatuation ends?

7. Rank these qualities in order of their importance to you when considering someone to marry:

- ___ Is Humble
- ___ Is Forgiving
- ___ Resolves conflict in a healthy way
- ___ Knows how to communicate
- ___ Prays
- ___ Is skilled in the art of friendship

12

SOMETHING YOU MUST AGREE ABOUT

One of the saddest scenes my wife and I have ever seen took place at a resort wedding. We weren't invited; we were merely spectators. But the context was as obvious as it was painful.

We were in Cabo, Mexico, on the Sea of Cortez. An hour or two before sunset, workers began scooping out a large heart shape in the sand, set up a table next to it, and surrounded the heart with lights. They sprinkled the heart with rose petals, and a little while later a middle-aged woman (we're thinking this was a second wedding) walked down the walkway, alone, toward a solo man standing in the heart.

There were no witnesses except for another tourist couple who had been asked to fill in. Their casual dress contrasted with the beautiful white dress of the bride and the white clothes of the groom as they stood facing the ocean. The sun was setting, the private table for two looked enchanting—it all seemed so romantic.

Two hours later, Lisa and I saw the bride, still in her dress, still carrying her flowers, walking alone. It seemed odd. She had gotten married about 120 *minutes* ago; why wasn't she with her new husband? Maybe she had something she just needed to pick up.

We said "congratulations." She smiled and moved on.

We walked around the grounds some more and saw the bride again about forty-five minutes later, walking down another hall, still alone, still in her dress, still carrying her flowers. This time, there was no smile. The tightness around her lips, the tension in her neck, the grip on her flowers gave it all away.

She couldn't find her husband.

This marriage was less than twenty-four hours old, and already someone wasn't acting like a husband.

Maybe there was an innocent explanation, a simple misunderstanding, but clearly this bride was a little embarrassed and more than a little frustrated.

How do you expect your spouse to act, not just on your wedding day, but throughout your marriage? One issue I've noticed that fewer couples address today concerns gender roles. Women, do you expect your husband to "act like a man," or does that very phrase offend you?

For your grandparents there was little, if any, disagreement on gender roles, but it's now become controversial. The problem is, while gender roles within church and marriage are discussed thoroughly in seminaries, few dating couples are aware of this issue and fewer still discuss it. In fact, the younger generation (I realize that many of you reading this may be as old as I am) has been brought up to treat gender distinction with the same disgust as racial discrimination. While I have my own opinions on this matter, what's probably even more important than whether you agree with me is whether you agree with each other on where you stand. If you disagree on this issue, I think it's a deal-breaker.

One of the top complaints I hear from thirty- and fortysomething wives is that their husbands aren't acting as "spiritual leaders," but some now question that very concept as inappropriate. Different views of gender roles are based on what theologians call "egalitarian" or "complementarian" views of marriage.

In general, the egalitarian viewpoint sees no such thing as gender roles in marriage. In this view, God doesn't call men to servant leadership; that's cultural conditioning more than it is scriptural. Every couple should make their own decisions about who does what best, divide up the responsibilities, and base their marriage on individual strengths and weaknesses. The husband isn't expected to be a leader but rather a fifty-fifty partner. The thought of him leading is, in itself, somewhat offensive and demeaning to his wife. Nobody has the final say, and neither partner has more responsibility than the other to provide, guide, and protect. Every verse that seems to suggest men have a leadership role at home or in the church can be explained away by context, later additions to the original manuscripts, a more refined study of the original language, or a "trajectory" view of Scripture that suggests the New Testament realized the first century wasn't ready for egalitarianism, so it simply laid the foundation for it in future generations. The fact that the church used to think that men needed to step up as leaders at home and in the church is a historical weakness that needs to be discarded and explained away, not a biblical truth to be applied today.

In the complementarian viewpoint, God has given the husband a role of loving servant leadership. Reasonable complementarians believe that the Bible describes this role more as one of *responsibility* than *privilege*, however. The husband essentially becomes a living *martyr* in his commitment to and service for his wife (Eph. 5:25–33), and she becomes his helper. Part of the man's martyrdom is lovingly leading her. This is what many—myself included—believe the Bible teaches in Genesis 3:16, 1 Corinthians 11:3, Ephesians 5:22–32, Colossians 3:18–19, and 1 Timothy 2:12–14, among other passages, taken together and applied throughout the majority of the church's history until the previous generation or so.

This is a matter of scriptural interpretation, but as a side benefit, I believe that the complementarian view seems to square better with recent findings in neuroscience about how the male and female brains work, as well as what makes for successful relationships. I frankly think the Bible is pretty clear on this, though there are a growing number of scholars (which, in fairness, I do not claim to be) who disagree with me.

This isn't the place to convince you of the rightness or wrongness of either position. If you want to study it for yourself, just google "Wayne Grudem" for the complementarian perspective and "Gordon Fee" for the egalitarian one, and you'll get more than enough information.

As I said before, what matters more than whether you agree with me, Wayne Grudem, or Gordon Fee is whether you agree with each other. Here's why.

WHY YOU NEED TO MARRY SOMEONE WHO AGREES WITH YOU ON THIS

The problems with disagreement on this issue may not be what you think. Many wives in complementarian marriages still manage finances. Many such husbands do much or even all of the cooking, just as many egalitarian husbands can be strong leaders. This debate often gets muddled by superficial, nonbiblical issues that aren't concrete or even helpful. It's often sidetracked with silly stereotypes—as if all complementarian men are abusive chauvinist pigs and all egalitarian men are spineless effeminate liberals. The last thing I'd call Wayne Grudem is abusive (the guy left a prime teaching position at a prestigious school to go to a then no-name college in order to serve his wife's physical health). I've been a teaching assistant for Gordon Fee, and he is, I assure you, neither spineless nor effeminate nor wishy-washy when it comes to biblical authority.

Most of the common misconceptions about gender roles aren't at a biblical level. Who handles finances, who cleans and cooks, who chooses where to go on vacation, or even what will constitute 99.9 percent of the general household decisions— biblical gender roles don't usually speak to such issues. But the notion of gender roles does affect marital expectations, how to raise children, what church you will attend, and how one views Scripture, all of which matters *deeply*.

A woman who expects her husband to be a spiritual leader and yet marries a man who finds such a concept demeaning to women and therefore offensive is going to find herself in repeated unresolvable conflicts. When finances get tight, for instance, she might expect him to step it up and get a better-paying job. He might think, "Why don't I stay home and *you* get a second job?" If your husband doesn't even believe in spiritual leadership, you can't expect him to become a spiritual leader. If that's what you really want, at least marry a guy who has that mind-set.

Guys who feel called to lead in their home but aren't allowed to do so will feel emasculated. Women who want their guys to lead but marry guys who don't will feel frustrated. Women who strongly adhere to the egalitarian perspective but who marry complementarians may not feel respected and will have serious problems when it comes to how the children are raised.

In a mixed egalitarian/complementarian marriage, both the husband and wife will likely try to treat the other according to their perceived sense of marital duties, but those duties won't be received as such—they'll be resented. What a complementarian woman finds loving and respectful, an egalitarian woman might find demeaning and frustrating, and vice versa. Since this rises to the level of biblical application, it must be frustrating to the extreme to aspire toward something that your spouse finds offensive.

People who disagree on this issue can still worship the same God, but it will be difficult for them to raise the same kids or operate the same household.

YOUR CHANCE FOR A "DO-OVER"

Because I believe that God designed marriage in part to make us holy even more than to make us happy, I also believe that He designed marriage in part to confront the pride of both men and women. In the complementarian worldview, men have their pride challenged in marriage by being commanded to put their wife's needs and comfort above their own (Eph. 5:25–29). Suddenly, another person not only has a legitimate claim, but a *prior* claim, on a man's time and money and affections.

The Bible challenges the pride of women by telling them to learn how to love their husbands and be a helper to them (Titus 2:4, among others). The Bible doesn't tell women in general to submit to men in general, but rather specific wives to submit to specific husbands.

The complementarian model, in my view, builds on this soul-shaping reality of learning to die to ourselves. It will help each partner grow in humility, service, understanding, and selflessness. It's a spiritually rich climate for potential character growth in Christlikeness.

Avoid rejecting the complementarian mind-set simply because you've seen it abused. A husband who claims "privilege" is a husband who doesn't understand the meaning of the word *martyr*. My daughter went through a college class that discussed gender roles, and her response was intriguing. "Dad," she said, "if most men treated their wives like I see you treating Mom, and most brothers treated their sisters like Graham treats us, more women would be complementarians. Most women want to be treated like that. But that's not the case. A lot of people my age have seen a lot of unhealthy marriages, and they don't want that. I think most women want what you and Graham offer, but they're rejecting what they've seen in their own homes."

I say this not to exalt my son or myself; there are a million things I could have done better as a husband and father. But I want you to seriously consider this: when you get married, you get a chance to create an entirely new family. Don't let unhealthy family-of-origin issues unduly shape the construction of your new immediate family. In essence, God is giving you an opportunity for a "do-over" *based on His Word*, not your experience. (I know there are some rich, deeply intimate, God-honoring egalitarian marriages as well. Obviously, I can only speak from my family's experience in this case.)

A woman whose father neglected her and focused only on providing financially for his family often finds herself drawn to the poetic guys who are in touch with their feelings. Unfortunately, such guys often haven't yet realized there's not a big financial future in poetry. After marriage, she'll soon forget about how emotionally available he is and be frustrated with how economically incompetent he is. It's one thing to date a guy who's "into" you when you've been neglected by your dad; it's another thing to have your financial future tied to his. This doesn't mean you should marry someone just like your dad, with all his faults—far from it. Just don't let an unhealthy pattern from your past dictate your choice in the future, *especially as a reaction*. Have your mind washed by Scripture, allow your heart to be cleansed by God's forgiveness and acceptance, and aspire to make the healthiest, most God-honoring choice possible. You didn't choose to be born into your family; you *do* get to choose who you marry to create your next family.

There are going to be some moments in your marriage when the two of you just flat-out disagree with each other. You'll talk it over, table it, pray about it, come back and talk about it again, and perhaps *still* disagree. In an egalitarian model, I suppose you could hire or appoint an arbitrator. In the complementarian model, if the man wants to be a biblical husband, he'll seek wise counsel and then put his wife's needs and concerns above his own. Ultimately, however, in such rare occurrences it falls on him to make the choice. In Lisa's and my twenty-eight years of marriage, there have been just two such moments. (In case you're interested, Lisa now fully agrees with the first call I made, and the jury's still out on the second.)

Gender roles are much broader than these uncommon quagmires, however. How are you going to raise your daughters? What values will you instill in your sons? This issue goes down to the very core of a person's identity. In my view, it also directly affects the way you read, study, and view the Bible, but that raises other contentious issues I don't want to get into right now.

The point is, you really need to come to some kind of agreement about this before you get married. Study it. Reflect on it. Pray over it. Come to a firm conclusion. And then make no compromise if you don't agree. As I said before, nonagreement on this issue should be a deal-breaker.

One more crucial point: ultimately, this is a biblical issue more than it is a matter of what you want. It's not appropriate to ask, "What role sounds better to me?" Rather, you should ask, "What scriptural perspective seems clearest?" After you reach that conclusion, find a believer who agrees with you. Some issues can be compromised on; this one shouldn't be.

STUDY QUESTIONS

1. Were you familiar with the words "complementarian" and "egalitarian"? Now that you've read about them, which one do you believe most closely resembles what you believe marriage should be?

2. Do you need to do more study to determine what the Bible teaches in this area? How can you go about that?

3. Discuss the most likely problems that will erupt if a complementarian marries an egalitarian, or vice versa.

4. How might these views affect the way you would raise and train your children? Are you willing to compromise on this?

13

YOU'RE LOOKING FOR A
COMPLEMENT, NOT A CLONE

I must have heard at least a dozen married couples tell a large group how it's impossible for two people to be more opposite from each other. In heaven, I hope God will put all of them (for surely, through the ages, there have been hundreds of professional speaking couples carrying the same message) in the same room and let them battle it out for supremacy.

They always come to the same point: they still have a really good marriage even though they're not technically "compatible." The danger in you thinking this way as a single is that there are different *forms* of compatibility, and some forms matter much more than others. It's worth considering this issue since lack of compatibility is one of the most frequently cited causes of divorce (even though I don't think that's really what is behind most divorces).

It's typical for opposites to attract, so don't worry about that. Compatibility that matters isn't about sameness as much as it's about having the most important things in common, beginning with a shared vision for life. Sincere appreciation and genuine respect for your future spouse matter far more than similarity.

Here's the challenge you need to overcome as a single who wants to know if you and your intended are compatible: the process of dating and looking for a mate, combined with the early days of marriage, provide an *artificial* sense of compatibility. If you're both looking to get married, if you both want to start a new home, if you both want to raise a family, those aims alone will take you through engagement, to the wedding, and through the first five or six years of marriage. Those are common goals that will give you something to talk about and build your life around. I can't prove this with any scientific study, but it's my belief that this in part explains why so many couples suddenly declare "incompatibility" even though they obviously once thought they had found their perfect match in each other. They've simply come to the end of this false compatibility and realize they have very little common ground with which to forge a new life together.

Let me explain. In the early days of your relationship, compatibility is artificially enhanced via sexual chemistry. Infatuation and immediate attraction are so strong, compatibility or incompatibility barely even register. You both feel crazy about each other—how could you *not* be compatible? And then when you move toward marriage and start planning a wedding, the ceremony itself gives you something in common. You plan it, talk about it, and divide up tasks to make it happen. After the wedding you start setting up a house, move into a new apartment or neighborhood, and try to join two lives. That also joins you in a common task and gives you something to talk about. If this is a first marriage, sooner rather than later you're likely to start raising kids. That's a big thing to have in common and requires a lot of communication. But eventually—unless you have about a dozen kids or space five kids five years apart—the kids are going to leave the two of you alone together. That's when the abundance or lack of compatibility will either take you to new heights or appear like a giant sinkhole that sucks the life out of your relationship.

The empty-nest years slay a lot of marriages, because the couple has slowly grown apart. They may never have shared that much in common other than having once "fallen in love" and gone through a few common life tasks while sharing the same address. With improved medical technology, many empty nesters have another twenty-five to thirty years left to live after the last child leaves home.

That's a lot of life, a lot of marriage, to share.

The good news is that when Matthew 6:33 is a shared value, you are spiritually compatible, and that's enough to hold a marriage together. However, other forms of compatibility will certainly make the relationship more *pleasant*.

RELATIONAL COMPATIBILITY

The foundation of relational compatibility is a shared appreciation for each other's *personality* and *character*. My wife isn't like me, but I *like* who she is. There are many areas in which I'm glad she's not like me. What would be a problem is if those areas annoyed me or caused me to disrespect her.

When it comes to evaluating relational compatibility, authors Ben Young and Samuel Adams remind us that personality doesn't change; we grow and evolve, but we don't become completely new people. So don't expect that to happen after marriage. *The person you marry is the person you're going to be married to.* That sounds elementary, but a lot of people don't believe that. They fall for a person's *potential*, thinking that the person they're marrying is going to change into someone who is substantially different. They thus marry someone with whom they might be somewhat "incompatible," hoping that, sooner rather than later, they'll *become* compatible.

Do you want to be married for the rest of your life to someone who sets your teeth on edge? Who embarrasses you? Who you are afraid to take out in public? Don't laugh—people do this all the time. They marry someone who does some or all of the above because they think it's time to get married, or they think it's the best they can do, or they get infatuated and rush into an ill-suited marriage—and soon resent who their spouse is. Then they try to change them.

Good luck with that.

Finding someone you enjoy being with is far more important (and less narcissistic) than finding someone who is just like you. According to Young and Adams, "It is not necessary or even healthy to find someone with the same personality traits. The issue has to do with your ability to accept and adapt to your partner's personality style, assuming it will not change."[1] In other words, you're looking for a complement, not a clone.

You can be an introvert who is happily married to an extrovert, as long as you like the fact that your spouse will be the life of the party. It will be a good thing if you want to be challenged to get out a bit more. If you never want to go out with others, if you are embarrassed that your partner derives energy from engaging (sometimes loudly) with others, you're best off not joining your life with his. As Young and Adams put it, you want to bring out the best in each other, and I think that requires mutual *respect* and *appreciation*. If you don't respect and appreciate your partner, you're not compatible. You'll never become a true, heartfelt companion of someone who bugs you, consistently embarrasses you, or for whom you have little (and dwindling) respect.

I know you love your boyfriend or girlfriend. But do you also *like* them? Are they the kind of person you enjoy being around? If it wasn't for the sexual chemistry, and if you didn't feel romantically inclined toward them, would you still enjoy their company?

Companionship is the relational heart that pumps blood into your marriage. People are often drawn to each other through sexual chemistry, and while there is a certain excitement in this aspect of relating, you'll be companions 95 percent more than you'll perform as sexual partners. Furthermore, sexual chemistry rises and falls far more wildly than does relational companionship, which usually grows deeper over time. Two companions can have at least a satisfactory sexual relationship if they are motivated by kindness and love. But a satisfactory sexual relationship does *not* guarantee relational compatibility.

Remember, you're seeking someone you are *eager to live with*, not *put up with*. If you feel like you are already tolerating your partner's personality for the sake of the relationship mainly because your feelings for them are so strong, proceed with caution. Marry someone you want to be married to for the rest of your life, not someone you hope to transform into a satisfactory spouse in five years' time.

RECREATIONAL COMPATIBILITY

There is a level of sameness that can be helpful, however, and that's in the area of how you like to play and relax. Most people can't afford to go on numerous expensive vacations. Maybe it'll be different for you, but here's where compatibility can become a serious issue. Lisa and I are friends with a couple who go to Saint Martin every year. That's what they do. They lie in the sun for hours, get a massage in the afternoon (*every* afternoon), have an early dinner, and call it a day. They might do one or two "activities" in the course of the fourteen days they spend there, but no more than that, and only if they want to.

Such a vacation—especially going to the same place and doing the same thing every year—would drive my wife bonkers. She lands on an island and thinks, "How can I explore every last blessed inch of this place in the mere 336 hours I have left?"

It's not just vacation—it's how you spend your evenings, weekends, and holidays. When both people really enjoy antique shopping, or gardening, or scouring bookstores, or following their favorite football team or NASCAR driver, or want to be at church as much as possible, or run marathons together, that kind of common activity *increases* intimacy as time passes. Shared interests fertilize commitment, satisfaction, and communication.

Here's the reality: life usually separates couples. Few married partners work together, so most of us are required to be apart from each other during the most active hours of the day, at least five days a week. If you also have to be separate in order to fully enjoy your rest and recreation, when are you going to connect? And can you truly connect when you don't really like what your spouse is most interested in?

Older remarried couples tend to do a bit better in seeking out compatibility in this area, in large part because they have more experience. A lot of twentysomethings don't really know what they like to do on vacation in the midst of working a full-time job (it's not until you're traveling thirty weekends a year that you can decide whether you'd also like to add traveling onto vacations). This is a tough one to imagine, so I'm downplaying it a bit for the younger crowd, but it's certainly something to consider and talk about.

ENVIRONMENTAL COMPATIBILITY

To stimulate your thinking and discussion, consider these three real-life scenarios of how couples found themselves in heart-wrenching situations where one or both partners had to make some serious compromises that they never considered before they got married.

A fiftysomething man was a leading prospect from his party to run for president of the United States. His wife didn't want to move to Washington, DC, nor did she want to endure such a nationally public stage. Though advisors urged him to run, though people circulated petitions asking him to run, though numerous pundits said he very well could win if he ran, in the end he didn't become a candidate. His closest friends and advisors gave one reason for his decision: his wife's opposition.

Rebecca steadily rose through the ranks of a company until she got an offer she never even imagined would happen: a prime executive-in-training position at the national office. Her employers were clearly grooming her for a VP spot sometime in the future. There was one major problem: her husband planned on taking over the family business in the south, and Rebecca's company expected her to move to Chicago. She and her husband had never talked about this possibility before they got married: when the reality of achieving their dreams collided, who got to pursue theirs first?

A young couple asked me to referee their disagreement. He wanted to go overseas to do missions work. She didn't.

"You guys have been married how long?" I asked.

"Nine months."

"Didn't you talk about this before you got married?"

"We thought we had...."

I can tell you this: if you marry someone who doesn't want to go overseas, *they will win that argument every time*. You just *can't* force someone to go overseas and expect the marriage and ministry to prosper. If God has called you overseas, it is your spiritual duty to marry someone who has some experience overseas so that they know what they are signing up for. Otherwise, you are being a poor steward of your life call and putting it in jeopardy.

All three of these scenarios contain a common truth: your spouse will have enormous veto power over where you live and what you do. Right now, all you can think about is just being together, but the time will come, sooner rather than later, when simply being together isn't enough. You will care passionately about what you're doing when you're *not* together—your forty- to sixty-hour workweek.

If you're both on career tracks, for instance, what will happen if those tracks take you in two different directions? Surprisingly enough, couples rarely talk about this, assuming "it will all work out." I've been asked to referee too many of these scenarios to believe that's true, so let me ask you: have you talked about where you might live, what you might want to do, not just in the next few years but also a couple of decades from now? Have you been absolutely honest about what you'll *never* agree to do or where you'll *never* agree to live?

Choosing where you'll live goes far beyond international/ national discussions, of course. There is a vast difference between a life lived in Manhattan and one lived in Coeur d'Alene, Idaho. If you were born in the Midwest and can't imagine another life, respect that. Some Midwest girls fall for a city boy and, in the abstract, living in the city can sound romantic and exotic, but when they actually try to live in a one-room apartment that costs more than their parents' mortgage did, breathe dirty air for six months, hear sirens blaring all day (and all night) long, pass panhandlers every time they go to the grocery store (which they have to walk to, or take public transportation to get to, and carry the groceries home in their arms), they start to go crazy. Similarly, a guy who revels in city life—restaurants being open at all hours, the energy that never dissipates, the ever-full menu of entertainment options—would pull his hair out trying to live in a suburb that essentially rolls up the streets at 7:00 p.m.

There is nothing morally superior about wanting to live on a farm, in a city apartment, or in a house in the suburbs. But if you don't agree, that's a pretty major challenge to overcome. Talk about this as a couple. Even better, to keep things honest, if you haven't talked about this, write down your preference before having this discussion, and then pass the papers to each other. It could be an eye-opener.

If you haven't ever lived in the city, and your potential spouse is set on it, do yourself a favor. Rent an apartment for a few months and try it out. You won't know, you can't know, until you do it, if you can stand it. Similarly, if your spouse dreams of a suburban lifestyle, try moving to a small town or the Midwest on a trial basis. Having lived in the Pacific Northwest, the Washington, DC, area, and Houston, Texas, I can attest that those are three *very* different lives.

It's far better to move somewhere on a trial basis as a single person to try out the option than to get married first and *then* see if you like it. I know, doing this can be expensive and it will slow things down, wedding-wise, and maybe you're already eager to get married. Even so, this is such a significant compatibility issue that it is worth delaying the wedding and paying whatever it costs to make sure the two of you are environmentally compatible.

WHAT ABOUT THE KIDS?

The roar sounded like a riot. Biking through the streets of Maastricht in the Netherlands, my wife and I thought we saw a street protest coming our way.

"What do you think we should do?" Lisa asked me.

"Ride toward it to find out what's going on, of course."

The crowd grew larger and louder; the air was filled with electricity. As we got closer, we laughed. An elementary school was ending its day, and hundreds of kids were being picked up by dozens of mothers for the walk home.

There's something about being on the other side of the globe, in a town you've never been in before, and seeing something so intimate going on—kids running into their mothers' arms, speaking a language you can't understand but don't need to, that makes you celebrate life as God designed it. The kids were showing off artwork, explaining how they got a hole in their pants, talking about an upcoming test. It wasn't difficult to figure out what they were saying, even though we didn't understand a word of it.

Put political correctness aside for just a moment. Men, if you want your kids to have a mother who greets them at the end of the school day and walks them home, make sure you marry a woman who wants that too. Women, if you want to be that mom, make sure you marry a man who shows the economic capability of affording you that freedom. If you want your husband to be the one at home to greet the kids, you better talk about that as well. Are you both okay with that little kid running into the arms of a nanny or grandma?

Who is going to raise your kids? Are both of you committed to being home by a certain time and keeping the weekends free? (If so, that will keep both of you from accepting certain jobs.) Is one of you okay with being home alone with the kids on occasion?

How do you envision the weekends: yard work or fun activities? That's going to affect what kind of house you buy. After kids arrive (or *will* kids arrive?), would you like to live in the city or suburbs? Have you always dreamed of foreign travel, or would you prefer to use limited vacation time and funds to spend time with your parents? Will you spend Christmas and Thanksgiving with your own kids or extended families? Okay, *which* extended family? Would you prefer to attend a large church or small church? Why? What if your spouse says "house church" or "no church"?

Do you value family meals or watching the news on television while you eat? Have you talked about your kids' education—homeschooling, private schooling, public schooling, sacrificing for college? Lisa and I gladly scrimped on retirement savings to put our kids through three private colleges; the majority of our friends (and every financial advisor we talked to) thought our doing so was fool-ish. It's no big deal to disagree with your friends on this; it's a huge problem to disagree with your spouse.

PUT IT ON PAUSE

I know—this is a *lot* to discuss and think about, but that's partly what dating is for. Now I'm going to ask you to do something that may feel even more painful: when you get close to becoming engaged, put any public announcement on delay for a few weeks and spend several sessions talking through all these issues *again* with someone else present. The reason I say this is that couples who are in love have an amazing ability to hear what they want to hear. Remember the would-be missionary who *thought* he and his wife had talked about living overseas?

Bring up anything you can think of. An occasional disagreement won't doom the relationship, so don't be too scared. But consistent incompatibility, in major areas, that can't be resolved is something you'd be foolish to ignore. You need to find a third party who loves you enough to point out these incompatibilities as they arise.

If you compromise on too many of these issues, or even on one really big issue, you risk fighting resentment for the rest of your life. I've talked with some of those couples, and believe me, you don't want to become one of them.

Remember: there's not one right choice. You don't have to make this one relationship work if it's not a very good fit. It's not wrong to want a certain level of happiness; in fact, it's wise to pursue general compatibility. However, while incompatibility is grounds for break-ing up an engagement or dating relationship, it's *not* biblical grounds to pursue a divorce. If you make a foolish choice here, the Bible is going to ask you to live with the consequences. Why not seriously examine your compatibility *before* you take the vows, instead of after? If you know this issue has broken up hundreds of thousands of marriages—*that, indeed, it's the most often cited reason for couples who are getting divorced*—don't you want to make sure it won't be a major challenge in your own marriage?

STUDY QUESTIONS

1. How common do you think it is that some people marry someone for their potential—who they might become—rather than for who they really are? Do you think people will change substantially (in fundamental ways) after they get married?

2. Why do you think it's important to marry not just someone you love, but someone you *like* and *respect*? What are the dangers of marrying someone who regularly embarrasses you?

3. How important is recreation time to you—evenings, weekends, vacations, and holidays? How important are various activities to you on those days? Are there any that you wouldn't (or shouldn't) be willing to compromise on?

4. Do you think two people could enjoy a marriage in which they have little in common, interest wise, on the weekends or on vacations?

5. Twenty years from now, is there anywhere you absolutely do *not* want to live (city, suburbs, rural, foreign country, etc)?

6. Do you envision one parent staying home with your kids, using day care, hiring a nanny, or trying to equally balance careers and child rearing? What arrangement(s) would *not* be acceptable to you?

7. If someone starts to recognize that they are making many compromises in order to consider someone they are romantically
   inclined toward, how can they work through their concerns in a
   responsible way?

14

WHAT YOU DON'T KNOW REALLY CAN HURT YOU

Dating can be a dangerous dance, with each partner focusing on the wrong things and actually inhibiting the development of a mature relationship. Unless you're thoughtful about how you date and what you do on your dates, they won't give you much of a clue about each other. Going to the movies, biking through the park, eating out—of course that kind of activity is going to produce and maintain a certain level of affection. But it's not real life; it's often not even real relating. It's just playing. It doesn't tell you squat about how a man could face a medical or vocational crisis, what kind of courage a woman has, what values each person lives by, or what spiritual pursuit drives the other person. Instead, you find out that you both like vegetables on your pizza and movies that have a plot—that's something, I guess, but it's not much on which to base a lifetime decision. It's okay to have fun. We *need* to have fun. But some dates also need to be purposeful, designed to ferret out your boyfriend's or girlfriend's character.

Let me approach this from another angle: women, any guy can fork over forty dollars to buy a dozen roses, but *not* any guy is truly generous and unselfish toward others. One romantic present, given with mixed motives, reveals nothing about a man's true character. Men, you can find women who will take off their clothes, but can you find a woman who will bare her soul so that the two of you can become one? Or is she so hurt and troubled that she'll lie and cover up anytime you get close to the truth of who she is, maybe even using sex as an escape valve to avoid truly relating to you or dealing with conflict?

Your mission is to truly get to know this other person—that takes intentional effort. Here's what to do to get there.

TRINITY TALK

Women, if a guy is more eager to undo your buttons than he is to listen to you share your heart, you're going to be very frustrated with him as a husband. Joshua Harris said it so well: "You can't love what you don't know. You can't be truly loved if you're not truly known. And the only way to know and be known by another person is to communicate—openly, honestly, sincerely, humbly."[1]

A young blogger interviewed me about marriage just after Lisa and I had celebrated our twenty-seventh wedding anniversary. She asked me for the one piece of advice I'd give. That kind of question is tricky, because it largely depends on the day you ask me. In this instance, though, I said, "Couples have got to stop with the secrets."

The truth is, we want to be known; we truly do. But we're afraid. If you see the real me, will you run away? Am I even worth being known? Will the real me bore you? Scare you? Repulse you? And so we hide. We start trying to please the other person more than we try to get to know them. We aim to get them to like us, rather than intentionally help them to truly understand us. In such a "dance" we never become truly known and thus live with the anxiety that if we do become known, our partner might leave.

Friends, do you want to live with those very natural and common fears *for the rest of your life*, or do you want to find someone who really does know you, accepts you, and still loves you? The only way to get there is to talk.

Now, the mistake so many young couples make is that they think sharing is confessing past dirt—sexual histories, abuse, broken families, previous hurts, etc. That's part of self-disclosure and something that should be done (with great discretion) at an appropriate time. By "appropriate time" I mean this: if you think your relationship could lead toward marriage, you want to discuss this before you become engaged (but after you've proven this person's character so that you know you can trust them with such intimate information). But this kind of confessional talk quickly falls off. Once you've shared a past hurt, it's shared; there's nothing more to say. And when your disclosure and intimacy are built on *past* events, what will you talk about after all your events are known and they're now mostly experienced together? This is when so many married couples *stop* talking and *start* hiding. (The two usually go hand in hand, by the way.)

You know why so many relationships slowly wither into nothingness? They stop seeking first the kingdom of God. There's no overarching mission in the couple's lives beyond self-enjoyment. This entraps them in a life of petty battles and superficial cares. If a woman spends far more time picking out a refrigerator/freezer than she does getting to know anyone who is spiritually lost, or becomes virtually consumed with getting a better office with a better view, that's not going to captivate any man for very long. When a man is obsessed more with becoming a scratch golfer than with being available to God, how could a woman not lose interest sooner rather than later? People grow bored with each other. They share what they've done and what they've experienced, but then they have no grand passion energizing their current existence. When we live for ourselves, we become boring. Most of us are simply not interesting enough on our own to captivate someone else for five or six decades.

What's the antidote? Seeking first the kingdom of God—not as a means but as an end in itself. Such a pursuit cultivates a fundamentally different form of sharing, the kind that comes first from relating to God. I call this "Trinity Talk." When we pray and read Scripture, God reveals Himself to us. We see our motivations in a new light; we see sins, but God reveals them to us in the light of grace. We can humbly admit our weaknesses and gain a vision for a better future. We are energized to attempt great things for God. We *never* run out of things to talk about because we are becoming new people with new visions and new purpose. Instead of sharing small, stagnant lives that produce little personal growth and even less vision, we become dynamic people who are growing ever more like Christ and are regularly reignited in our passion to see God's work spread in the world.

My good friend Kevin Harney had been married for a number of years when God spoke to him about becoming "recklessly generous" toward a church-based need. He swallowed hard as he considered the actual amount he believed God was calling him to give. That much money would mean emptying out virtually all of their life's savings.

When he came home from work, his wife, Sherry, explained how, during her morning jog, God had prepared her to "give generously" to the same project. She gulped and mentioned a number, fearing Kevin's reaction. It was the exact same amount that her husband felt God had placed on his heart.

While this episode depleted their bank account, it filled their marital intimacy to overflowing. They were risking for God, growing in God *together*, facing the excitement of life on the edge of serving God *together*. The last thing you would say about Kevin and Sherry is that they are bored with each other.

It's not just about what we do for God; it's about who we become in God. When I keep relating to God, I literally become a different person, so there's always someone new for my wife to get to know. The same is true for me with her. Just recently, my wife prayed a brilliant prayer for some hurting parents. The Spirit of God within her was so mightily evident it renewed my love for her all over again, and I thanked God for the privilege of being married to a woman who is growing in the grace of prayer.

Living by the gospel provides the security so necessary to build a foundation of mutual fellowship. I've had times of prayer when God has revealed just how sinfully or pitifully I've been acting or feeling, but He does it with such assurance and grace and in the provision of Christ that I come out of the conversation feeling washed, blessed, built up, and strengthened. I might be really messed up, but even more importantly, I know I'm really, *really* loved. When I know that I'm so deeply loved by God, I'm willing to be more vulnerable with my spouse, and I'm more willing to attempt something risky for God.

Such ongoing spiritual insight and mission are exciting to share, but they presuppose that we're growing in the Lord. If God wasn't in my life, facing my sin would be much too terrifying and embarrassing to let anybody into my inner world. I wouldn't want my wife to see my sin without the hope that there is One who can change me. And I could never come up with worthy dreams on my own. I'd be obsessed with small-minded thinking related to my comfort, affluence, "success," and reputation. Boring!

I don't think I'm capable of being known or knowing someone else apart from the hope of the gospel. Because of God I can forgive others when they sin against me, I can love others when they act unlovable, I have a place to go to get rid of my resentment, and I have a reasonable source of hope for those who need it. Quite frankly, God also gives me something worth saying.

My point is that your communication needs to become three-way: bring God into the center of it. What is God revealing, what is God doing, what is God forgiving, counseling, encouraging you with? If I'm with someone who doesn't even know God, I'm going to run out of places to explore sooner rather than later. Their personal development will be limited to human wisdom and insight.

On your dates, find out what God is doing in and through your friend. Do they even hear from God? Are they aware of their sin? Are they hiding from their current sin? Do they have any sense of mission?

By the way, it's much easier to admit *past* sin than it is to admit a current struggle. Is every weakness that your boyfriend or girlfriend is sharing from some distant age, but never anything they're struggling with now? Since we know from Scripture that "we all stumble in many ways" (James 3:2), if your boyfriend or girlfriend isn't working on something or aware of something in the present, they're simply not reading Scripture, and they're not listening to God. And if they won't listen to God, why in the world will they listen to you ten years from now? You might be fascinating, but you're not half as fascinating as God.

In short, I want someone actively relating with God, so that she can actively relate with me. I can't find this out on top of a Ferris wheel or watching LeBron James drive to the basket. We've got to be alone. We've got to talk. Not just about the past or her family or her fears, but about what God is doing in her life *right now*, what He's forgiving her for, what He's calling her to become, what He's inspiring her to do.

WATCH WITH ME

A young man lost a chance at employment when he went out to dinner with a prospective boss. As soon as the waiter put a plate in front of him, the young man salted his food and started eating. The boss was blunt, and perhaps unfair, but said, "I don't hire people who salt something they haven't tasted. I want you to know what's going on before you try to fix it."

That might seem trivial to you, and maybe it is. I'm just making a point from a real-life example: when you're with your boyfriend or girlfriend, *pay attention*. How do they treat their family? What's their relationship like with their parents? Their siblings? How do they act around kids? How do they treat "invisible" people—waiters, janitors, and the like? If a guy is too lazy to bus his own table at McDonald's, what makes you think he won't leave his stuff around the house, expecting someone else to pick it up?

Here's the painful reality when you enter any dating relationship: your partner can't be completely 100 percent altruistic. That person just can't. She wants something from you. Maybe he wants to marry you. Maybe she wants to make out with you. Maybe he just wants to make you like him. You can assume that she's on her best behavior with you. So whatever your boyfriend or girlfriend does *for you*—buy flowers, bake food, offer encouragement—comes from somewhat mixed motives.

The only way to know true character, then, is to watch your friend with someone else. Women, if you're with a guy who wants to be in ministry, but he's criticizing every pastor and every sermon he hears, I guarantee you that five years after he's married to you he'll have a whole lot of criticism about your role as a wife. Guys, if you're around a woman who does kind things for you *but no one else*, the days of her doing kind things for you are severely numbered, probably within weeks of the wedding, if you want to know the truth.

Choose dates that will test your boyfriend or girlfriend. Sprinkle this season of your relationship with impromptu "interviews." Get into ministry situations, family situations, maybe even stressful situations, to see how he or she reacts. If one little thing goes wrong and ruins the whole date, you can bet that on a future family vacation there is going to be a whole lot of drama and not much rest, because something always goes wrong on a family vacation.

Most modern dating focuses on how two people treat *each other*. That's not particularly helpful, especially in the blush of infatuation.

You've got to get outside the relationship to get inside the motivations and heart of the person you're thinking about marrying.

GO DOWN MEMORY LANE

Keeping with this theme—how to test a serious dating relationship—now try to explore what your boyfriend or girlfriend was like *before* meeting you. Did he enjoy sports, did she attend church, did he do the things the two of you enjoy doing together now? Without letting on what you're doing, purposefully try to crack the code of your beloved's past, as that past is a fairly good indicator of the future.

Infatuated couples invariably try to change for each other. Remember, during infatuation you become obsessed with getting and keeping your heart's desire. Because you so desperately want the relationship to work, you will find yourself astonishingly open to making little compromises and temporary changes in your lifestyle and even personality to accommodate the relationship. This motivation almost always fades with the infatuation. If your future spouse didn't go to church before he or she met you, it's unlikely church will be a priority after the wedding. If that person pretended to like sports, or museums, or cooking, it won't take long until the playacting ends. *Get to know your potential spouse's past so that you can get a read on your future.* Be very suspicious of any major change.

Talk to his or her siblings, parents, friends. Ask to see old photo albums. You've got to be a bit discreet here—don't sound like an FBI agent interrogating a witness. But informally drop a few questions in the middle of casual conversations to get just a little bit deeper into your potential spouse's psyche.

As you consider these and other issues, I'd recommend my friend Dr. Paul Friesen's book *Before You Save the Date: 21 Questions to Help You Marry with Confidence*. Going through Paul's book will assist you in getting inside your partner's heart.

PRAY

At the start of the Boston Marathon, everybody looks the same. Sure, there are different ethnicities and genders, but people tend to have a certain "look"—or they wouldn't be able to race there. This makes it difficult for spectators trying to locate a loved one. At the prerace expo, which is wall-to-wall people, my daughter said she almost called about a dozen different men "Dad." She saw a Boston coat (which you don't see that often in Bellingham, Washington), a certain body type, and a man wearing a baseball hat and assumed it was me—until the guy turned around. In my hometown—in that getup, anyway—I look distinct. Here, I looked like everyone else.

During the race, however, people begin to distinguish themselves. A woman asked me my time the next day, and when I said "3:31" she replied, "Oh, you're much faster than my friend. He was 550."

"Do you mean he *placed* 550th or that he finished in five hours and fifty minutes?"

"He placed 550th."

"Ma'am," I said, "there was a wall of humanity between your friend and me at the finish line. He is *way* faster than I am."

We might have *looked* alike, but we didn't *run* alike.

In the same way, dates can "look" alike, but get them alone before the Lord of the universe, hear the concerns of their heart, and you can get a better read on who they really are in Christ. How do they talk to God? Is He their friend or some distant stranger they almost seem afraid of or embarrassed by? Do you pick up a heartfelt passion, a sense of someone who is familiar with this conversation, or do you feel like you're listening in on someone who is talking to you and trying to impress you more than actually talking to God?

What does she pray for and about? Does he have a concern for others, do her prayers reveal a trivial life and petty concerns, or is he swept up by God's compassion for others?

Are you praying with someone who is comfortable being silent before God, listening to God as you would in any other conversation? Or is he in a rush to just impress you and move on, afraid that silence or a lack of eloquence will make him look bad?

Most of all, does it sound like this person has been here before, or is all this just a show? Of course, people can still "act" when they pray, but if you pray with them more than a couple of times, you'll begin to get a better feel for where they're at with the Lord.

PUT IT ALL TOGETHER

So, to wrap all this up, how do you really get to know your potential mate?

- You engage in Trinity Talk. Move beyond the superficial and historical to the present and future. Don't just talk about your past; talk about what God is doing in the present and what you think He's calling you to do in the future.

- Watch that person in his or her natural habitat—at work and home; with family, friends, and strangers.
- Take a walk down memory lane, with other loved ones as tour guides. Find out what your future spouse used to be like.
- Pray with him or her. Someone might succeed in lying to you, but it's a little trickier to present a false front to God.

STUDY QUESTIONS

1. Since most of us want to be known and to truly know someone else, why do we so often hide from each other and even mislead each other in romantic relationships?

2. How might a "current grand passion" keep feeding a marriage? What are the dangers of marrying someone without such a shared passion?

3. How important do you think it is for someone to be not just a Christian but *growing* as a Christian? How can you tell if someone you are dating is stagnant or maturing?

4. What are the dangers of someone who freely shares past failings but never current struggles?

5. Do you think it's fair to suggest that the way a man treats his sisters and mom might reflect on his character as a husband, or the way a woman treats her brothers or father might hold clues to the kind of wife she would be? In what ways?

6. Are there dangers involved in dating partners praying together? What might be some of the benefits? How can this be done appropriately? (Or should it?)

15

A NEUROCHEMICAL WAR
AGAINST YOUR REASONING

Sami and Danielle got legally married early on a Sunday morning in Houston, Texas. They didn't have sex until Wednesday night, about eighty hours later.

Let me explain.

The young couple planned to get married in Mexico, but Mexican law requires a Mexican clergyman, Mexican blood tests, and a certain period of time in-country for the wedding to be legalized. Sami and Danielle wanted to get married by a pastor from their church, Second Baptist, not a clergyman they had never met. So they had a short legal ceremony performed by the Baptist pastor, signed the papers, and caught a flight for Mexico.

Danielle told her new husband, "This doesn't mean a thing until my daddy walks me down the aisle."

Sami wasn't quite as eager to waive such informalities. He had signed a legal document. A pastor he respected and loved had declared him married. He was paying for a great honeymoon suite at a resort in Mexico, so why, on Sunday, Monday, and Tuesday night, was Danielle sleeping alone in that beautiful, spacious room designed especially for romance—and he was down the hall, sharing a small room and even a bed with his dad? To make matters even more painful, Sami's father decided to use these final hours they had together to dispense "marital advice" in anticipation of the big day.

I'm not asking you to discuss whether Danielle should have given Sami a room key. Though it was more than a little frustrating for Sami—he had already waited so long—he admits in hindsight that it was "special" waiting until after the formal ceremony. But you might be thinking, "Isn't all this a little outdated? Come on, this is the twenty-first century! Nobody waits until they get married anymore."

I want you to look at sex and dating in a way that perhaps you never have before. You have heard the sermons and read the biblical verses about not mistreating each other: "It is God's will that you should be sanctified: that you should avoid sexual immorality; that each of you should learn to control your own body in a way that is holy and honorable, not in passionate lust like the pagans, who do not know God; *and that in this matter no one should wrong or take advantage of a brother or sister*" (1 Thess. 4:3–6 NIV 2011).

That alone is reason enough not to get involved sexually before you marry. But understanding God's purposes for sexuality should reinforce your commitment. God knows what He's talking about. His plan is brilliant. The more I think about sexuality and study God's purpose, the more amazed I become about this incredible invention that He designed—and the wisdom He dispenses in telling us how to use it.

If you scope out a female brain, you'll find that a woman may have up to ten times more oxytocin running through it at any given time than your average man. Oxytocin is a neurochemical* that creates or at least reflects feelings of warmth, affection, bonding, and intimacy. And the fact that women have more of it explains a lot about their general comfort with relating to others emotionally.

There is one time, however, when a male's level of oxytocin approaches that of a female. Immediately following a sexual encounter, the man experiences a surge of oxytocin that may even catch him off guard, which explains why single gals are sometimes shocked when a man they barely know blurts out "I think I love you" following a hasty sexual encounter.

Within marriage, this flood of oxytocin is a brilliant attachment device. God knows infatuation can open our eyes to notice someone, but He also knows those feelings will fade. After we're married, we need something that will renew our affection for each other on a regular basis. One of the most hurtful things young wives tell me is that they resent how before the wedding they seemed to be their husband's number-one priority, but after the wedding they dropped to number three or four. There's just something about the male psyche that after we "get the girl" we move on to the next challenge. Suddenly, the new husband is focused on his career, his golf handicap, his hunting, his fantasy football league, you name it.

---

* Technically, it's a "neuropeptide."

God is not unaware of this. He knows we men are not altruistic by nature and may grow to ignore our wives. Since our wives are also God's daughters—and God is passionately devoted to His daughters—He very ingeniously created a hormone (we call it the sex drive) that healthy men carry plenty of. And He designed marriage with the instructions that the only legitimate place sexual satisfaction can be found is with one's wife. So the husband has a literal physical reminder, "I need my wife," and when that need is expressed and met according to God's explicit instructions, the man's brain is flooded with a bonding neurochemical that reignites his affection and passion for his wife.

Again, within marriage, this is brilliant. A wise man soon learns that to be sexually intimate with his wife requires maintaining emotional and spiritual intimacy as well, so he has a physical drive that can keep him from getting complacent relationally (unless, of course, he turns to a cheap substitute such as pornography).

However, outside of marriage, what proves immensely helpful to *cement* a relationship proves equally unhelpful to *test* a relationship. If your infatuation is fading, but you're sexually intimate, you're renewing your neurochemical affection for each other. You're learning to draw that intimacy from each other and assigning that feeling of intimacy to each other. Yet you're still in a relational stage when you should be testing and evaluating the relationship, not cementing it. Even apart from the moral aspect, premarital sex is a foolish thing to do for this reason: just when you need to be most alert to make the best choice you can possibly make, one that will affect you and your future family for the rest of your life, sex creates a neurochemical fog that will confuse you. You're going to feel like you want to stay with that person, even if you mentally understand that it's not a particularly wise match. *You're literally launching a neurochemical war against your mental reasoning.* Dr. Paul Friesen boldly stated, "There is no area that blinds couples more to their challenges than premature sexual involvement."[1]

Any way you look at it, sexual involvement before marriage is unhelpful. If the relationship proves unworthy of a lifetime commitment, having been sexual will make the breakup more painful. It will dull your ability to sexually connect with the person you do marry. And it will confuse you as you evaluate the relationship. When you sexually reconnect, you feel the effects of the neurochemical cement. Learning to *disregard* this cement (which you must eventually do to break things off) will undercut the positive effects it has in marriage. You must train yourself to ignore what God created you to pay attention to.

The notion that this doesn't matter as much as trying out your "sexual compatibility" is ridiculous. God *designed* sex to be pleasurable and satisfying. He knew what He was doing, and no surprise, He succeeded. Sex can indeed be amazing. It's also a skill that can be learned, and that's what marriage allows, so if the two of you aren't "compatible" on your wedding night, you have a lifetime to get there.

Two people who genuinely care for each other and who are growing in the virtues of kindness and generosity will figure out, sooner rather than later, how to please and keep on pleasing each other. You don't have to "test" sex—believe me, it works! Enjoying sex with each other isn't a test of the relationship—that's like saying, "We know we were made for each other because we both think chocolate chip mint ice cream is delicious" or "we both think sunsets are beautiful." Join the club—so do billions of other people. In the same way, plenty of people could potentially bring you to the point of orgasm. And guess what? You'd enjoy those orgasms. God created you with skin, nerve endings, genitals, and a brain that makes sex supremely pleasurable. In the end, all you've learned is that God is a good Creator and engineer. You haven't learned whether the person who manipulated your body to orgasm is capable of building a family with you.

Of course, staying sexually pure isn't easy. If your partner is a good potential match, it's going to be excruciatingly (and increasingly) difficult to stay sexually pure. If it's not difficult, in fact, you should take notice. I love how my friend Paul Friesen described this: "Some couples will boast that the physical purity part of their relationship is going well. 'We have no problem in this area,' they may say. If you have been dating for a while and are contemplating marriage and 'have no problem in this area,' you have a problem. You should be fighting with all your might to stay pure—there definitely should be a strong sexual desire for each other."[2] The absence of sexual desire could be a serious indicator of underlying problems.

According to statistics, it's likely that you and your boyfriend or girlfriend have already been sexually intimate with each other. You might be thinking, "What now?"

Immediate sexual connection, like infatuation, fades. It puts you in a fog for a while, but couples who are sexually intimate break up all the time. I'm speaking here apart from the spiritual context, which we'll get to in just a moment. For the purposes of evaluating your relationship, decide from this point on that you're going to do it God's way. You're going to stop what you've been doing and see if the relationship grows or suffers accordingly.

We also need to consider, which we'll do now, how to respond to a sexual past with someone other than the person you're considering marrying.

WILL OUR SEXUAL PAST STEAL A FULFILLING FUTURE?

Writing this section is difficult because I'm going to make some of you very angry. It's going to sound like I'm telling people not to marry you. I hope you won't read it that way, but rather, if you have been promiscuous, you'll consider the advice along the lines of what you need to do in order to become a better candidate for a godly marriage.

First, a caveat: there are almost no single adults left in this world with a "perfect" sexual past. For instance, various studies show that 80 to 90 percent of people who get married aren't virgins. I don't know how accurate these studies are, but when you add in sexually related acts that fall short of sexual intercourse but still result in orgasm, and then things like pornography, strip clubs, and even just a lifetime exposure to hard-core cable television, the reality is that most of us stumble into marriage with a decade's worth of sexual brokenness, at least. You will have to look long and far to find a person who doesn't have some sexual stain in their past.

This universal dilemma doesn't mean that the *level* of a person's prior sexual involvement doesn't matter. It does. It's something you're going to have to deal with in marriage. Sin can be forgiven, but it does have consequences. It corrupts our minds, trains our brains and bodies in the wrong direction, and needs to be fought against. When talking to couples I have noticed a direct connection between a woman's level of sexual promiscuity and the sexual difficulties she has in her marriage. It doesn't have to be this way—we'll talk about why in a moment—but it often is, largely because people feel so ashamed of their pasts that they rarely deal with it. They just pretend the past didn't happen or act like it won't matter and then suffer the consequences accordingly, without ever drawing a line of connection between the lack of healing in their past and their sexual performance and enjoyment in the present. If there weren't consequences to sexual sin, it seems unlikely that God would forbid it. He is a gracious God, not capricious, definitely not malicious, and amazingly kind and generous. Directly rebelling against His wisdom, doing nothing about it, and then expecting there to be no consequences is worse than calling God a liar; it is calling Him a pleasure-killing, malicious liar.

We can face these very painful and embarrassing issues and look boldly at our sin, admitting its ugliness and its past power over us, precisely because God is *not* a liar. In fact, we have confidence to face the reality of our brokenness because we serve the all-powerful, victorious King Jesus who died to cover the cost of our sin and who sent His Holy Spirit to guide us into a new way of thinking, a new way of feeling, and a new way of living. Without such hope, denial and moral "tolerance" would be the only polite response. With this hope, why settle for anything less than God's best? Jesus *died* to win this hope, to create this reality. The least we can do is embrace it. God can and will defeat the stain and effect of our foolish, sinful choices.

THE PORN PROBLEM

Women, here's one of the challenges you face: because of the rise of the Internet during your boyfriend's generation, exposure to pornography is barely south of universal. Almost every guy has seen some, and many guys have seen a lot. The producers of porn have dramatically shaped the souls and expectations of millions of single men.

First, I feel sorry for your boyfriends. When I was growing up, you had to be a certain age (sixteen or eighteen—I can't remember) to buy one of "those" magazines at the store. Today, the Internet offers salacious material freely, without making even a token attempt to protect young minds. I hope you understand that this isn't a fair fight. Take any twelve-year-old boy, naturally curious, and tell him, "Press this button and you get to see what a naked woman looks like," and he can't push that button fast enough. It might not even be prurient—there's just a natural curiosity at play. Then tell him, "Now, press this button, and you'll get to see what sex looks like," and his curiosity will once again get the best of him. Some boys, exposed to something their souls aren't prepared to handle, will get a rush like they've never known before and will then be ushered into a habit that will stick with them for perhaps the rest of their lives. Curiosity did more than kill the cat; it has captured a generation of boys. God's judgment is certain for those who wage war on young minds like this, enticing them and making it so easy for them to go against their conscience. I feel for your boyfriends.

There's an even more sinister side to all of this. Studies show that porn is sort of like marijuana, in that both have a tendency to be progressive in a certain percentage of cases. About 5 percent of people who use marijuana will graduate to heroin. Interestingly enough, about the same percentage—5 percent—of pornography users will become sexually violent to the point that they actually commit a crime. The 5 percent of each category don't know who they are before they dip their toe in those waters. They won't find out until they open the floodgates and watch themselves get carried away into actions that, prior to their exposure, they would have found repugnant. And of course there are various degrees of damage between committing a sexual crime and having a polluted attitude toward sex in general.

Thus, a young boy's natural curiosity, cruelly exploited and cleverly targeted, can lead him to enter a world where his view of sex is warped and his soul is bent. And a small percentage of boys will eventually become sexual criminals. Any way you look at it, this is an evil world.

If you are dating a guy who has an extensive past of watching porn and who, even now, can't stop it, you ought to be concerned for a couple of different reasons. One, his expectations have been jettisoned to a dangerous place. He's trained himself to think that women like to do certain things, actually enjoy certain things, and act in certain ways that bear zero resemblance to reality. There is zero "soul connection" in the world of Internet sex, and connection is the only sexual expression that truly satisfies long term. If you can't ultimately satisfy the customer, you have to shock him. If you can't get him to bond with someone familiar (as God intends sex to do), you have to make him obsessive about seeing something *new*, something *different*, every time, something even more whacked-out than what he saw last time. And thus the spiral toward more deviant forms of sexual expression continues.

Listen, *healthy* sex is extremely pleasurable in every sense of the word. You don't have to try weird things to make it pleasant and keep it exciting. Two people who are connected relationally, emotionally, and spiritually, with bodies that function the way God made them to function, can have tremendous sex without resorting to unnatural or demeaning acts. The Bible gives tremendous freedom to a husband and wife to enjoy and pleasure each other in many creative and exciting ways, so there's no need to get evil in order to get excited.

A guy steeped in pornography has had his mind warped to the extent that he needs newer and perhaps kinkier thoughts and acts to reach the same level of excitement. Contemplating fifty to sixty *years* of sexual activity with such a mind should make you cautious, as that's a long time to go a long way in the wrong direction. Furthermore, if he watched commercial* pornography, his soul has been shaped into a selfish morass where it's all about the guy getting pleased. The whole concept of sex as a gift to be given is obliterated. His thoughts will be, "Am I getting any tonight?" Women who sleep with guys like this tell me they feel "hunted," "used," and even "treated like a masturbatory magazine." That gets really old really fast.

On a spiritual and neurological level, guys who have a long history with pornography and multiple sexual partners are less able to bond with one woman sexually. They've trained their brains to connect sex with *women in general*, not *one woman in particular*. One of

---

* I'm already going to get in trouble with this chapter, so let me step in it some more. Women, there is a difference between the *kinds* of pornography your boyfriend may have been exposed to. Some is bent beyond belief and proves to be far more damaging. This is something a counselor needs to help the two of you work through.

the prime purposes of sex—rebonding husband and wife, recementing that marital affection—is compromised.

A year ago, after hearing me speak on sex, a young man in his twenties married to an attractive young woman of the same age confessed to me that, all things being equal, he actually preferred masturbating to pornography over having sexual relations with his wife. He was ashamed of this, he hated that this was so, but giving in so many times had made him actually prefer fake, imaginary sex over intimate relational sex. He hoped marriage would "cure" his problem, but all it did was expose it.

People, we shape our brains. We cultivate desires, habits, and addictions. Repeated actions, over time, make us who we are. God can intervene, restore, and re-create, but He doesn't do that on the back of fraud and denial. He heals through the practice of confession, repentance, and the applied blood of Jesus Christ. Anything less won't cut it. Even after forgiveness, however, the brain still often struggles to let go of the patterns of the past. Forgiveness is one thing; sanctification (walking in holiness) is often something very different. Even after a guy is forgiven, it will take time for his brain to be rewired in a healthy direction.

Which is why, if you're a guy with a significant history with pornography (to the extent that you've tried to stop watching it and always fail), seek professional-level healing *now*. Go to a counselor who knows what he's doing. It's worth the cost; it's worth the embarrassment. A sexually fulfilling marriage is priceless. Dealing with your past to make that possible is one of the best investments you'll ever make. Don't let Satan steal a lifetime of satisfaction from you by telling you that because of your past you don't deserve sexual fulfillment in the future. This has nothing to do with what you *deserve*. It has everything to do with what Jesus *bought* on your behalf.

One of the dangers for women to be on the lookout for (which is why rushing into marriage is risky) is that some men, when they become infatuated, will stop looking at pornography for about a year, but when the infatuation fades, they'll go back to it. I'm not speaking as a trained psychologist who can explain this, but rather drawing conclusions from anecdotal confessions. Several men have told me that the early days of marriage and sexual activity with their wives kept the porn compulsion away for just less than a year or so. When sex became routine, the old urges came right back. Instead of spending the effort and time to work on their marital sexuality to make it more fulfilling, they found it all too easy to fall back into old patterns of self-pleasuring.

Which means, women, if you become sexually active with your boyfriend before he's your husband, and he's had a long history with pornography, you don't know how true his healing really was. He might say, "I haven't looked at it since we've met," but how do you know that in another few months, once sex with you becomes a little more routine, he won't go right back to it? If you become sexually active and marry him within less than a year of meeting him, you're hoping that he really is healed, that he won't go back, and that he's not (God forbid) in the 5-percent category hurtling toward a sexual nightmare.

To be safe, you want to see him have at least a year or two of victory over this sin, without having sex with you to hold him up. Then you'll know he has the strength to stand firm when temptation strikes after marriage, because it will. If he has a history with it, he will struggle, to some degree, for years to come.

Keep in mind: just because sex is pleasurable doesn't mean it's easy. You will have some issues to deal with to build a mutually satisfying sexual relationship. You don't want to be married to someone who will take a lazy shortcut to avoid having to work on a real relationship. If a guy's only sexual outlet is his wife, he'll be more inclined to work on the issues as they come up rather than ignore them.

ARE EX-STRIPPERS SAFE?

Guys, you don't just marry a woman; in one sense, you marry her past. If you focus on a woman's outward appearance and not her character, you're likely going to marry a woman who suffers from many *more* poor choices in her past (certainly, many beautiful women make great choices—I'm not warning you away from beauty, but rather pointing out the necessity of making character a priority). A therapist friend of mine has worked with a number of different women who were at one point in their lives centerfolds for popular men's magazines. These women often had difficulty achieving sexual satisfaction. Though they seemed experienced in sexuality per se, they had almost no understanding of God-ordained sexual intimacy within marriage. As a result, there was a lot of spiritual and psychological healing that had to be accomplished in order for them to enter into a mutually satisfying relationship. They had connected sex with power and money. When sexual intimacy was supposed to become real and all about building intimacy with a man they cared about, they found that the road back to true relationship was very difficult to find. How frustrating it must be to be married to a gorgeous woman yet unable to connect with or satisfy her sexually.

The same could be said of strippers who, in essence, become actors for money. After a couple of weeks they slip into a routine and learn to look at men as "marks" who show signs of providing the best tips. It's manipulative, it's chilling, but it's a fact. When you connect sex and acting for a living, night after night pretending to like a guy because you want to persuade him to buy a lap dance, how can you ever build a genuine relationship of true intimacy and honesty?

But here's the good news. My friend Dr. Steve Wilke has spent tens of thousands of hours in clinical therapy and has seen numerous couples healed of sordid sexual pasts. He often shocks couples who come in for counseling when he talks to a woman with a colorful history and tells her that she's a virgin.

She says, "Yeah, right, a 'spiritual' virgin, I get it ..."

Dr. Wilke replies, "That's not what I mean at all. I mean this potential spouse could be your first one."

The couples' jaws drop open. "What are you talking about?"

Dr. Wilke goes on to explain that they have never had *real* sex as God designed it. "It's always been about money, power, and manipulation. Neither of you has ever surrendered yourselves in a relationship where you are truly loved, cared for, and protected, and where there is spiritual covering through prayer and the Word. You've never known Song of Solomon or garden of Eden sex. This will be the first time that you have ever experienced sex in the context that God created for both of you to enjoy. You have no idea how different this kind of sex will be."

To be fair to couples in these circumstances, Dr. Wilke suggests that getting there requires a tremendous amount of spiritual and psychological clinical work so that the couple can replace the old habits with new ones. Potential mates with clinical backgrounds and histories should prepare for marriage with a trusted professional to learn to love in God-honoring ways. You might think that meeting with a professional sounds extreme, but if you're really messed up, it's not like changing a flat tire on your car—anyone can do that—it's more like rebuilding the engine. That takes expertise. The comforting news is that Dr. Wilke has seen the gospel of grace heal men and women in ways that reflect how Christ loved His church so that they can actually experience sex on their wedding nights as "virgins" according to the full extent of God's sexual plan for us.

If a woman knows she is forgiven, understands the grace of God, and is loved by a man who is spiritually, relationally, and emotionally in tune with her, she will usually melt in his arms. Her past won't vandalize her future. The one exception is if there has been a moment or moments of severe sexual trauma—that takes a little more therapy.

Which means, couples, that if either of you has a past that would make not just your mother, but even Oprah, blush, you need to seek the best counsel money can buy before you ever consider marriage. Furthermore, without working out the past "through fear and trembling," no couple can expect the sexual fulfillment that God intended as a realistic expectation. If you do your part, sexual enjoyment is a realistic expectation. On the other hand, if you think saying one little prayer will wipe out a decade or more of misbehavior, you're fooling yourselves and will be banging your heads against a wall as you try to build a healthy sexual relationship.

It comes down to this, for both men and women: past sexual sin has consequences that often must be overcome even after forgiveness. If the person you're thinking of marrying has dealt and is dealing with their past in a healthy, mature, and gospel-centered manner, you can proceed with some degree of confidence. If you catch them lying to you or making promises but not doing the mental, spiritual, and physical work necessary to be fully healed, the marriage bed will eventually become one of your least favorite places on this earth.

A SACRED TRUST

One of the things I love about marriage is how God calls two broken people together and secures a covenant relationship that supplies the necessary stability for two people to heal and grow (seeking righteousness). You need to count the cost, however, in determining how much healing your future spouse needs. Before you get married, it's essential to discuss your sexual past—not in overly vivid detail, but with enough disclosure to give each other an honest appraisal of the issues you'll be facing after marriage. Let me put it this way: if I got married concealing a hundred-thousand-dollar debt, a serious health issue, or a prior felony that made future employment problematic, everyone would admit that I had committed an act of fraud. In the same way, a future spouse deserves to know how much effort it's going to take to participate in God healing your sexual past, in part to ascertain how much healing you've already initiated and how much healing he or she is willing to be a part of.

My friend Ally Vesterfelt, who got married while I was writing this book, dated a man who broke up with her before she met her future husband, Darrell. That man told her that her sexual past was "too much for him to handle." Looking back, Ally said, "At the time I thought his assertion was a horrible denial of God's grace, and I ridiculed him for it (privately). Now I see it as God's provision for me. Darrell doesn't feel burdened by my past, and I don't feel burdened by his. We have been honest about it, and we both feel ready to embrace one another's shortcomings, whatever that means. We're committed to 'walk it out' with each other to wholeness and healing."

If, after sufficient exposure to your intended's past, you believe the person is healed and healing, it's not unwise to marry him or her. Once you make that decision, however, if you want to be a redemptive force in that person's life and experience Song of Solomon sex, *you must let their past go.* Author and pastor Joshua Harris was a virgin when he got married. After his future wife confessed to him her premarital promiscuity, Joshua's dad told him, quite wisely, "You need to settle in your heart that you will *never*—whether it's in the heat of an argument or under any circumstances—use her past as a weapon."[3]

It is kind and generous to take on someone's debt when he or she becomes your spouse. It is cruel and petty to keep reminding that person what car you could buy, what house you could live in, or where you could go on vacation if only he or she hadn't accrued such debt. You don't have to marry a person with a complicated past. If your potential spouse hasn't dealt with that past in a healthy way, in fact, I recommend you don't proceed into marriage. But if you do marry that person, you will undercut the security, intimacy, and stability of your marriage by *ever* using it as a weapon. If you don't think you can get there, don't marry him, don't marry her. This is one of those things where even one accusatory slipup can be very, very hurtful. Count the cost, but once you count the cost, you must let it go.

Sex is a powerful tool. In a healthy marriage, used appropriately, it can be nothing short of glorious. As people who believe God is the Creator of our bodies and our sexuality, we should be eager to embrace His good handiwork. But know this: the more powerful the tool, the more training and caution you need when learning to use it. That's what this chapter is all about—not scaring you away from sex, but helping you to take sex further than perhaps you ever could have dreamed, as a servant of your intimacy, a protector of your purity, a renewer of your relationship, and a very sacred place of pleasure.

STUDY QUESTIONS

1. Were you aware of the way sex affects us chemically and relationally? How should this knowledge affect the way you view premarital sex?

2. Why do you think the stereotype is that a couple is enthusiastically active sexually before the wedding, but then sex becomes boring just months into the marriage? Why do you think this happens? Can it be avoided? What can you do now, as a single, to not fall into that trap?

3. In this chapter Gary stated, "Any way you look at it, sexual involvement before marriage is unhelpful." Do you agree or disagree? Why?

4. Is it possible for a couple to know they are "sexually compatible" without having sex? Does this matter?

5. How important do you believe it is to know each other's sexual pasts? To what detail?

6. How can you determine whether a person is healed from his or her sexual past—either sexual promiscuity, pornography, or something else? What are some wise steps a person should take to evaluate if it is wise to marry someone with a particularly troubled past? What, in your mind, constitutes a "particularly troubled past"?

16

PROBLEM PEOPLE

If you've caught the vision for a marriage that seeks first the kingdom of God, you need to be on the lookout for personality traits that will undermine such a focus. I can't deal with every one—that would be a book in itself (and a rather depressing read at that). But let me focus on three serious problem people when it comes to choosing someone to marry: takers, people you can't respect, and "incomplete" people who aren't secure in their relationship with God. Other personality weaknesses might undermine marital satisfaction in general, but these three traits make a *spiritually prosperous* marriage more difficult in particular.

IS THIS PERSON A TAKER OR A GIVER?

All this focus about marriage being an opportunity to grow in love and learning how to love could be misunderstood if you're inclined to be a codependent person. A marriage of ministry is a marital *partnership*. Two givers geometrically increase their ability to give. A giver married to a taker gets depleted and tired, which is why you want to find someone who knows how to love and give. Such an ideal isn't selfish; it's wise. If you marry a taker, you'll compromise your own ability to love others outside the marriage.

The sad reality is, some people are givers and some people are takers. Givers don't always mind being in a relationship with a taker because they *like* to give; it brings them joy. But there are times when the giver needs to receive. Let's say the giver gets really sick, or is laid off, even though he provided the bulk of the income, or just goes through a discouraging time and suffers things he has never known before, like depression or anxiety.

In those instances, can your taker learn to give? In most cases, sadly, the answer is no. That person might freak out, abandon the relationship, or just run around in an emotional/relational panic, adding to the giver's problems rather than addressing them.

If you marry a taker, you're sitting on a relational time bomb, because you're making the bet that, as a giver, your fallen body and your fallen soul won't ever get *so* fallen that you'll someday need help, at least for a season.

That's foolish, because you will.

When a taker has to give, he feels sorry for himself even more than he feels empathy for you. Instead of concentrating on providing care, she'll talk about how difficult she has it, trying to get everyone to feel sorry for her.

I once spoke to a couple in which the husband had been a drug addict for ten years—their entire marriage. His wife had been out-standing in her care and patience. He finally submitted to God, was going through recovery, and asked me how "this *Sacred Marriage* stuff" might apply to him. I responded, "You have a great opportunity to begin giving back to your wife and serving her in a way you never have. She has put up with your addiction for a decade; now you can focus on serving her as part of your own healing, loving her as God's daughter, and asking God every day how you can love her like she's never been loved before."

"But wouldn't that be making her an idol?" he asked in all seriousness.

In my humanness, I wanted to throttle the man. His wife had demonstrated heroic patience and love toward him for *ten years*, and he thought giving a little back to her now might be *idolatry*?

But that's how extreme some takers can be. When a wife is giving birth to a child or suffering an illness, a taker's buddies hear only about how he's not getting any sex. When a husband who is the sole wage earner comes home, fixes dinner, takes care of the kids, and even cleans up the dishes, the taker wife thinks he's being selfish if he wants his twice-a-week bout of sexual intimacy (this is a real-life example, by the way), because she's tired from her tennis match.

Even if you're a giver who likes to give, it's exhausting being married to a taker. A taker will suck the life out of you in many ways, and in one sense undercut your ability to minister to others. You can still minister, but you'll have less energy to do so, because your marriage will be holding you back.

If God is calling you to a strong ministry outside the home, don't even think about marrying a taker. Part of being a good steward toward a ministry call is building a life that can support that call, and marrying a taker will undercut that. I have told some singles, as they have described the dynamics of their dating relationship, "If you marry this person, they'll become your primary ministry. You won't have much left over after taking care of them. Is this what you think God is calling you to?"

HOW DO I KNOW IF I'M DATING A TAKER?

A taker's response is always, first and foremost, about them. In an extreme form, if you're late for dinner or a date because you got into a car accident, a taker's first words will be, "Why didn't you call?" or, "So when can you get here? I feel like an idiot sitting here by myself," or, "Just call a cab or something and don't make me wait any longer." A giver would say, "I'm so sorry to hear that. Are you okay?" A giver would be more concerned about your comfort: "Don't stress; these things happen; what can I do to help you now? Do you need to be picked up?" Their thoughts will be about *you*, not about *them*.

Another mark of takers is that they will give when asked to but almost always ask for something in return. They have to get something out of the agreement before they will be satisfied. You say, "I really miss seeing my parents; do you think we could drive down next weekend and pay them a visit?" and he'll say, "Sure, as long as you_____." A giver delights in giving because it gives delight to his beloved. A taker negotiates an action for what he'll get back for himself.

It might sound selfish to want to marry a giver, but, as I've said so often, do you want your kids to be raised by someone who resents being annoyed, or by someone who will parent with a servant's heart? Do you want to invite someone to a home where your spouse is more concerned about the floors or furniture getting dirty, or where the guests feel welcomed? Do you want to sit in a restaurant with a date who treats the server like an underling or like a person who may need to be encouraged?

The person you marry will be married to you in every element of life. You're not just choosing a spouse—you're choosing a partner who will represent you, as half of a couple, to the rest of the world. Wouldn't you rather be part of a giving couple? Think about how much more you can give, how you can accelerate your family's ability to love others, when you join one giving heart to another.

Ask yourself, when you spend time with your partner, do you feel drained or invigorated? Would you describe the relationship as healing and supportive, or exhausting and combative? To you givers, asking these questions may feel uncomfortable, but here's where I want you to consider marriage as a base to seek first the kingdom of God. When you know that someone has your back and will help you out if you get into trouble; that the spouse waiting for you at home won't be as frustrated by your delay as she will be delighted that God is using you; that he will want to listen to what happened and help you recover, you're freer to serve others. You will also—somewhat ironically—have more energy to love your spouse if you're married to a giver rather than a taker, because a taker often uses up your energy in other ways, most notably by regularly demanding acts of performance. Takers thereby sabotage your ability to give love to them in a way that is satisfying and honoring to God.

WHEN RECEIVING IS GIVING

What I'm about to say might seem, on the surface, somewhat contradictory to all I've said before, but it's an important qualification. A true giver can also receive. I need to give; to be healthy and to honor

God, I need to serve my spouse. If my spouse won't let me serve her, I can't honor God or love her like I should.

So a true giver allows me to give back to her because she knows that I need to give, that it's not healthy for a relationship to become so one-sided. Receiving my love and service is actually an act of love. Jesus let His feet be washed. Jesus let His body be anointed with oil. Jesus let women support Him financially. Jesus received and receives Mary's worship and ours. Jesus let Martha fix His meal. Jesus let Simon help carry His cross.

Jesus is the greatest servant who ever lived, yet part of His servant nature was seen in Jesus allowing others to serve *Him*.

IS THIS A PERSON OF RESPECT?

As soon as you marry someone, you are biblically responsible to respect that person as your husband or wife. This will be much easier for you to follow if you marry someone who is respectable. Psychological studies mirror Scripture in this insight: people are happiest and most satisfied in their marriage when they are married to someone for whom they have a high level of respect. This is particularly true for kingdom-centered marriages.

If the person you are attracted to is not generally respected by people you trust and believe in, that's a real problem. True godly love, the love between two partners in Christ who are passionately pursuing service in God's kingdom, contains a high dose of mutual respect. And while you can choose to respect someone just because he or she is your spouse, the kind of respect we're talking about now is a respect engendered from a person's character and actions, not position. If you are going to grow old with someone, make sure it's someone you respect. If you're embarrassed by this person, if you constantly have to reassure your friends and family that "what he or she did (or said) might look bad, but it's not as bad as you think," you're setting yourself up for a frustrating marriage. Racism, prejudice, dishonesty, laziness, gluttony, materialism, selfishness—all these grow *more* unpleasant the longer you have to accommodate them. If you're already tired of having to excuse your partner of one (or certainly several) of these, you're going to have a tough time when it comes to marital satisfaction twenty years from now.

Besides, if you have to mop up after her for how she alienates people, how he neglects people or displays boorish behavior, how are you going to support or, even more difficult, join his or her ministry? You'll be so busy trying to clean up and apologize for the mess your spouse has made that you won't have time left over to break new ground together.

The three laws of real estate are location, location, and location. The three laws of marital choice for a ministry-minded marriage should be character, character, and character.

INCOMPLETE PEOPLE

If someone thinks getting married is the cure for being lonely, purposeless, or friendless, he or she is being very foolish—and you're being just as foolish marrying that person. *Marriage doesn't solve emptiness; it exposes it*, so marry someone who has a solid core. If someone can't live without you, he or she will never be happy living with you either.

In *Sacred Influence*, I spent a good bit of time reminding wives that "God, not your marital status, defines your life." The reason I said this is that spiritual security is an essential platform for the full expression of biblical love. If I'm not secure in my relationship with God—that I am accepted, loved, and empowered by Him—then I won't risk saying something or doing something that might make my spouse angry or frustrated. That's a huge problem if your view of marriage is two sinful people walking a journey toward increased holiness.

When I know I'm loved by Christ, I can bear others' disapproval. When I know God accepts me, I can act in a way I'm convinced is right, even if it angers my family or my in-laws, so I'm free to serve my wife first over them. When I am secure in God's approval, I won't become a child-centered spouse, neglecting my wife in a desperate search to make my kids appreciate me, because that need for acceptance will already have been met by God. I will be free to love and train my kids while still keeping my wife as my top priority.

Let me get really practical: are you more afraid of saying no to your partner's sexual requests that go beyond the bounds of propriety than you are afraid of displeasing and dishonoring God? Single men, as bizarre as this may sound, you need a woman who is so connected to God she will displease *you* before she will displease *Him*. A married woman who is motivated by God first even above her affection for you is a far superior lover, in every way (including sexually). Women, the same is true for you. If your man gives in to premature advances, or just as bad, pressures you in that way, he is demonstrating a failure to love.

Guys, if you marry a woman who is motivated by reverence for God over affection for you, she'll learn to be kind to you and affectionate toward you even when she doesn't feel like it and when you're acting like a jerk. The same thing that feeds her chastity—love and respect for God—will feed sexual enthusiasm within marriage. The same thing that feeds promiscuity before marriage—selfishness and fear—will kill sexual desire after marriage.

But this has far more to do with character than with sex. I want a partner in holiness. After reading a rash of stories of mature men in ministry who had some very sad episodes requiring them to step down from their positions, I pled with my wife: "Please, tell me if you see unrepentant sin in my life that I'm just not getting. I don't want to end up like that. And if I stubbornly refuse to listen to you, please take it to Steve or Rob [two close, lifelong friends] so that they can take it from there."

It would take a very secure woman to stand up to her husband like that. But that's who I want to live with. The Bible tells me that I am more than capable of being deceived by my sin, so why wouldn't I want to be married to a woman who can effectively counteract that rather than go along with it because she's too insecure to speak up? The thought of Lisa serving me like that is *comforting*, not *threatening*, because I know whatever she does will be done out of love.

Yet some of you are getting very serious about marrying a woman or man that you have to spiritually carry on your back, hoping they'll eventually find their own legs. Take a deep breath, think about the future, and proceed accordingly.

We've just addressed three problem *characteristics*. Before we close this chapter, I want to touch on a problematic *process* that could indicate someone has some more maturing to do before getting married.

YOU DON'T NEED A SIGN

What if someone has read up to this point in the book, believes he or she has found someone who wants to base a family on Matthew 6:33 and who has complementary marriage style expectations, thinks the person is a giver, a person of respect, and is someone who is rooted in God—but this particular reader still can't make up his or her mind, even after a couple of years of dating. Is that a problem?

It might be.

Some believers say they must wait for a "sign" from God before they feel "released" to marry. This entire book has challenged the claim that there is only one person to marry and that life is about finding that one person. We've demonstrated, scripturally, that the choice is up to you—both whether to get married and who you should marry (as long as they are a believer). Since that's the clear biblical teaching, if your partner insists on a sign, that's a good indication that your potential spouse likely lacks necessary confidence and the ability to make decisions. A good chunk of life is about making decisions: where to work, where to buy a house, when to have kids, who to make friends with, etc. What if he has to wait on a sign to have children? Is she going to have to wait on a sign to get a job? What if his job isn't meeting your family's needs, but he insists on getting a sign before being aggressive about finding a better job?

If I was with someone who had dated me for three years and said she still needed a sign, I'd say, "Okay, I understand. But I need someone who doesn't need a sign to make a decision, so I guess this is where our dating relationship ends."

Remember, if there's not just one person to marry, you can courageously move on to find someone else who is more suitable for you. My advice is that you find someone who is a giver, so that you'll be better able to give. Find someone who is respectable, and you'll be able to minister and break new ground together. Find someone who is complete in Christ, and you'll be better able to pursue a life of righteousness. Find someone who is more secure in his or her relationship with Christ than in his or her relationship with you, and you'll be blessed immeasurably. And find someone who is growing in the ability (and confidence) to make wise decisions—including the decision to marry you—and you're well on your way to building a God-honoring family.

STUDY QUESTIONS

1. Gary stated that some people are "takers" and some people are "givers," but isn't this a matter of degree? How can you tell if someone is primarily in one camp or the other?

2. How might accepting Jesus's words "Seek first the kingdom of God" affect your concern over whether the person you are marrying is a "taker"? Does this make such an evaluation more or less important? How so?

3. Do you ever find it hard to receive from others? How might refusing to do so sometimes be selfish?

4. Why do you think that when someone feels "in love" they are willing to stay with someone for whom they have little or no respect? What can we do to guard against this?

5. What would likely be some of the most common marital problems if you married someone who wasn't spiritually "complete," who felt like they needed someone else to complete them?

6. Would someone insisting on a sign from God before they get married make you more or less interested in them? Why? What do you think the Bible has to say about this?

17

WHY YOU WON'T KNOW YOUR WIFE UNTIL SHE TURNS THIRTY-FIVE

Greg* is an insightful, mature, godly Christian man who started a successful business. He married a woman from another part of the country and seemed to have an ideal Christian family with two daughters until his wife hit her midthirties and returned to her family of origin in the Northeast for a three-week visit.

When she came back home, she announced that she was now a smoker.

Greg was mystified. "What kind of person *starts* smoking at thirty-five?" he asked me.

I had no idea. I had never heard of this.

Then Greg's wife began watching wildly inappropriate cable television shows with their eleven- and thirteen-year-old daughters.

---

* Not his real name.

"Are you kidding me?" Greg asked his wife.

She called him "boring" and went out and got drunk with her friends. You have to understand: Greg had *never* seen his wife drunk before, but the first time he did, he tried to shield it from their young son (fortunately, their daughters were away that evening). And then he had to work through the excruciating reality that she had driven herself home.

Throughout the first fifteen years of their marriage, Greg and his wife had been on the same page regarding values, raising their kids, going to church, serving God, and making entertainment decisions. Suddenly it felt like they were on two different planets.

As surprising as these issues might seem, they were relatively superficial compared to other issues that arose. Greg spent three years trying to hold his marriage together with his "new" wife, but in the end, she got bored with him and left.

I've since heard of several such examples—spouses who take a serious turn for the worse not long after the kids get through grade school. I'm not a therapist or a trained psychologist, so this is just amateur speculation, but here's what I think is going on: some people from troubled backgrounds manage to pull things together—for a while. They put up a bold front long enough to get married. They hold things together long enough to have kids. They then hold themselves together long enough to get their very young kids into or through grade school, but as soon as those kids aren't quite as dependent as they used to be, the mom (or dad—it can go both ways) finally succumbs to whatever addiction, mental illness, or personality quirk they've been trying to repress for most of their life.

If you're a PhD personality detective, in hindsight you might be able to find some carefully concealed clues, but nothing that most people would catch.

In one sense, everything I've said in this book up to this chapter, taken out of context, could seriously mislead you. If you've heard me say, "Do your homework, find a godly spouse, and you'll have a wonderful, spiritually rich marriage until the day you die," you've heard too much. There's no guarantee. The reality is, people are dynamic creatures. Many people change *for the worse.* Some who seem to live for their faith in their twenties become ardent foes of the faith in their thirties or forties. Some people who remain virgins until they get married suddenly start acting up sexually fifteen years after the wedding.

It's really sad, but it happens.

I'm just trying to be honest.

Here's the thing, though: if marriage really is about *why* more than *who*, your mission will still be the same. Hosea was faithful to God even as his prostitute wife was unfaithful to him. Bathsheba became the mother of David's son, taking an honored place in the genealogy of Jesus, even though David took her when she was still married to another man and then murdered her husband. When it's *mission* first and *marriage* second, you realize you can serve God in a happy or a sad marriage, an unusually difficult or a (relatively) easy marriage.

Because there are no "right" people—in the sense that all of us will "stumble in many ways" (James 3:2) and are prone to sin—it's all the more important that we pursue marriage for the right reason. If the person becomes our primary pursuit and that person goes bad, where does that leave us? If we're driven by mission (which is, at the root, a relationship with God), then we will never lose our core purpose.

Secondly, if you marry for the right motivations, if you keep God first in your life, if you live by Matthew 6:33 and also seek, as Paul wrote, to be ever filled with the Spirit, you will never be alone in your marriage. You will face trials, but you won't face a single trial without God's comfort, guidance, and presence.

I say this because, absent the focus on mission, even the pursuit of a "godly" marriage can be a selfish one. Perhaps you want a godly marriage because you want a godly marriage's benefits, so you take your time, do your homework, apply due diligence, give God an opportunity to stop you, seek counsel from your friends, and get married with the attitude of, "God, I've done my part, now You do Yours: give me the marriage I want!"

It doesn't always work out that way. People are dynamic. They make choices. Our choices shape our character. Sin is corrupting. If someone—even a believer—starts deliberately giving in to a particular sin, it will eventually change him or her into someone different. You have no guarantee that this won't happen to the person you marry.

One of the main points of my book *Sacred Marriage* is that God can use the challenges present in any marriage to help us grow in holiness, learn to depend on God, and increase our ability to love. That's a glorious thing, if we recognize that we need to develop in all three of those areas.

I say this because I'm fully aware of the scare factor inherent in this book. I've painted some horrific scenarios, and the sad reality is they're all based in fact. But that shouldn't stop us from marrying with joy and even a measure of peace, assuming we act wisely, because we know that God will be with us all of our days. There is no perfect spouse to be found; even really good spouses will try our patience, will sin against us, and occasionally may deliberately hurt us. Yet God can do some wonderful things through painful and even horrible circumstances.

You see, marriage isn't just about finding the right person so that you can have a good marriage. It's also about becoming a better person, and anybody you marry can help you do that. My friend (and really good blogger) Ally Vesterfelt, who as I mentioned earlier got married while I was writing this book, read an early draft and offered some well-spoken comments:

> Look at your partner's flaws and think about if you can live with them, yes. Think about if you want that person to be a father/mother to your children, etc. But I would warn singles against blaming a bad relationship on the significant other. I think this sets us up for failure in marriage. I spent too much time as a single looking for a "good husband" and not enough energy thinking about what would make me a good wife.
>
> In my experience my partner's flaws have most often mirrored my own, even if I didn't realize it. If I am in a relationship and think, "Wow, my boyfriend isn't ready to marry because he has this glaring issue," chances are I have a similar glaring

issue. It might not be the exact same issue, but it will likely mirror my partner's. I worry about singles looking at a bad relationship and thinking, "Okay, all I have to do is break up and *look for another partner*." That won't fix their problem. Or at least it didn't fix mine.

It took three tragic relationships before I realized the problem was my own (I'm a slow learner). I kept thinking that if I could just get out of the "bad" relationship I was in I could find a better one—a better guy. And when the relationships kept being bad I still didn't see my role in it. I kept thinking, "Why is God against me? Am I like a magnet for bad guys!?" Three remarkably different guys and remarkably similar outcomes later, it occurred to me: wherever I went, there I was. Finding a better guy was not the answer. I had to confront what was going on with *me*.[1]

Those are wise words. Begin, even while dating, to see relationships as a path toward holiness, and you'll naturally apply the same principle in marriage. Relationships are God's way of working on *two* people, not helping you find the *one* person you want to spend the rest of your life with. You can get so obsessed trying to find the right person that you can mentally tear a decent but imperfect person apart. Or, afraid of what might happen, be too terrified to ever commit. I've probably contributed to some of that fear with the sobering tone of this book, but I'm going perhaps a tad too far in one direction because I see too many Christians not even considering some basic and potentially disastrous issues. If we truly understood all that marriage involves, every wedding would involve a certain amount of trepidation, if not outright fear.

But here's the hope: as Christians, we don't believe that a happy marriage is the primary goal of life. Glorifying God is. In most cases, God's glory is best pursued by making a wise marital choice and building a family that will honor Him. But remember Hosea, who, for the glory of God, was instructed by God to marry a prostitute who cheated on him, conceived children with other men, and all but broke his heart. Did he have a "successful" life? Absolutely. What about John Wesley? His wife quite possibly was mentally ill. Things got so bad that when she eventually abandoned him, Wesley wrote in his journal, "I didn't ask her to leave, but I'm certainly not going to chase after her." He had a disastrous marriage but also lived a supremely significant life. John Calvin had a fantastic wife—but she died barely a decade into their marriage, and he lived alone for the rest of his days.

Remember how we started this book? Seek *first* the kingdom of God. Not a happy marriage. Not an easy marriage. Not even a wise marriage. Those are all noble pursuits, but the *first* call of every Christian is to fulfill God's will for their life and to grow in righteousness. Most of us will not be called into a Hosea marriage, but some of you, even after making a careful choice, may well feel Hosea's pain of betrayal. This will hurt, but it needn't wreck or define your life if your spiritual priorities are in the proper order.

The truth is, no marriage is easy. There is no guarantee that the person you marry will continue to grow in faith. She may backslide. He may get sick or break psychologically or spiritually. But you'll be okay. And you'll grow in the process. That's a good thing.

So take a deep breath. God isn't going to leave you. Who you marry will affect you, but that person needn't define you. Don't lose your joy, wonder, or even happiness as you face this season in your life. Life is a journey walked hand in hand with God. We want to walk in wisdom, but God has plenty of experience helping His children work through the consequences of foolish choices (their own and others').

Embrace the soul-healing words of Christ: "And surely I am with you always, to the very end of the age" (Matt. 28:20).

STUDY QUESTIONS

1. How can the concept of "mission first and marriage second" help you face your marital choice more confidently?
2. In what ways could a person's pursuit of a godly marriage be rooted in selfishness?
3. How can you know, when dating, whether the issue is that the person you are dating is not mature enough to get married, or the issue is that you've got some personality weaknesses that keep getting exposed?
4. How can you properly evaluate someone as a potential marriage partner without tearing that person apart? How do you keep that balance between recognizing someone's strengths while also seriously considering weaknesses?

18

WHAT ABOUT YOU?

HOW WOULD JESUS DATE?

So far I've been encouraging you to put your intended through the spiritual equivalent of an SAT test. Keeping with the theme of the last chapter, though, let's ask, what about you? Are you dating with integrity? In your pursuit of a good marital match, are you acting with grace and kindness? Is the *process* of your search honoring God?

In the interest of full disclosure, I did a miserable job of this as a single, so I can't use myself as an example. Fortunately, we have a much more reliable source to turn to: Jesus. While Jesus never dated, He did have friends, and His friendships reveal the nature of His relationships in such a way that we can imagine how He would date.

John 11 is a great case in point. Jesus built a strong friendship with Mary, Martha, and Lazarus. When Lazarus grew very sick, the sisters sent word to the miracle-working rabbi to hurry back to

Bethany because Jesus's friend was close to death. Remember, doctors were all but useless then. Jesus was their *only* hope. Yet Jesus purposefully delayed His visit until after Lazarus's death.

It looked really bad on the surface. The Jews in Bethany had tried to kill Jesus, so Martha and Mary knew they were asking Jesus to risk His life to return. An uncharitable view of His delay might have been that Jesus was afraid. A slightly less uncharitable view might have been that Jesus was just too busy or indifferent to a close friend's need. Grief isn't always rational, and the accusations that later flew out of these women's mouths when Jesus did show up demonstrated their distrust.

As God, Jesus knew that His friends would feel betrayed. Even so, in the words of classical writer R. Somerset Ward, "He disciplined the natural impulse of his affection and waited."[1] Ward's language gets a bit archaic here, so let me paraphrase the rest: Jesus's friendship was so true that He put His actions above what His friends would think about His actions. He knew they would question Him, but He did what He knew was right anyway.

Is your friendship great enough to put your loved one's good above your loved one's opinion of you? That's a difficult place to get to, but it's the only foundation for mature love. You have to become the kind of person who does what's best even if the person you love doesn't think you're acting with the proper motive or concern.

According to Ward, such "unselfishness is only possible by means of discipline, of warfare with selfish desires. The highest bond of friendship is forged in the fire of discipline, and it is true to experience to say that the greater the cost of the forging, the greater will be the friendship."[2]

Most people think the highest bond of friendship is the fire of emotion and affection. What makes someone a friend in the modern mind is that we *like* or feel fondly toward that person. Ward suggested, and Jesus modeled, that the highest bond of friendship is personal discipline. Friendship is doing what's best for someone, even if what's best is confusing or feared or resented. To get to this place, we literally have to declare spiritual war against our selfishness.

Romance is built on loud and unreserved displays of lavish affection, but such displays can be evidence of an undisciplined heart. Sometimes the most loving thing to do is to limit your displays of affection by submitting to God's greater good for this person. Jesus could have immediately traveled to Lazarus and healed him—and never given Mary or Martha an opportunity to question His love— or He could have allowed Lazarus to die, allowed Mary and Martha to go through a natural questioning of His love and commitment, and thereby teach them a valuable spiritual lesson. Jesus chose the spiritual lesson and waited until Lazarus died.

It goes a little deeper than this, however. Jesus told His disciples that more than pleasing Mary and Martha and even saving Lazarus was at stake: it was God's will for Jesus to raise Lazarus from the dead. Jesus couldn't do that unless He first let Lazarus die. Jesus lived first and foremost for the glory of God, above every human friendship, and that made Him the truest friend any man or woman could ever have.

Jesus's decision to return to Bethany shows the courage of His friendship. Circumstances looked so bleak that His disciples thought He was committing Himself to a certain death. The disciple Thomas said to the other disciples, "Let us also go, that we may die with him"

(John 11:16). Jesus wasn't moved by the opinion of His friends or the threat of His enemies; He lived entirely to fulfill the will of God.

A DELIBERATE MAN

Notice how deliberately and purposefully Jesus acted in friendship, without regard to His safety or reputation. Let me ask you a tough question: when you see a friendship or romance just beginning to bloom, are you deliberate or impatient? Do you seek God's face before you "explore" your feelings and discuss them? If your feelings are contrary to God's will, they are, at that moment, irrelevant, if indeed Jesus is your God and not just your "friend."

Many couples tend to be undisciplined and hasty in declaring their affection. They rush in and blurt out their feelings before seriously even knowing the other person. And then they tend to be very self-centered, wanting the other person to respond in kind and begin meeting their romantic fantasies with equal desperation.

Jesus does the exact opposite. Ward pointed out that the mistake we often make in our friendships is that we "give too generously what is useless to our friend"—i.e., easy displays of affection—and then we are too stingy in giving the "more costly gifts," i.e., sacrificially reining in our feelings until we know we can back them up. He continued, "At the back of all appearances lies the truth that the measure of love is its costliness. To analyze one's feelings is the worst way of arriving at a measure of friendship; to count its cost is the best way."[3]

To analyze one's feelings is the worst way of arriving at a measure of friendship; to count its cost is the best way.

Jesus lived and taught that friendship and love are marked by sacrifice: "Greater love has no one than this, that he lay down his life for his friends" (John 15:13). Feeling romantically inclined toward someone but not mentioning it because you know doing so would be premature and unwise is one of the most loving and difficult things you will ever be asked to do. It is difficult to feel so strongly and not talk about it with the one you're infatuated with. And it is so delicious to hear that the feelings are returned. But giving free rein to such emotion and conversation is the opposite of love; it is selfish. It threatens that person's emotional and spiritual health. It shows a lack of concern, a lack of care, a total lack of the willingness to sacrifice on which true love is based.

Displays of public affection; verbal commitments that are born out of sheer emotion; false promises based on temporary emotions— these are the "useless" gifts that Ward says we can be so generous with. But then we're too stingy with the costly gifts essential for the other person's well-being: we don't consider his or her welfare before we pronounce our commitment or affection; we don't consider whether our displays of affection will be healthy or cause possible confusion and later hurt. Are you learning to deny your selfish desires and put the other person's spiritual welfare ahead of your own emotional and physical lusts?

How do you truly know whether you are committed to this person and that you truly love him or her? Here's how you know: analyzing your feelings is the "worst way of arriving at a measure of friendship; to count the cost is the best way." Your love is measured by your willingness to act unselfishly, to even let the person think less of you, if in doing so you are serving their spiritual advancement. If you would rather *not* declare your love because you want to make sure the relationship is wise, that's counting the cost. That's love. If you would rather know whether your feelings are returned before you even know whether the relationship would honor God, that's selfishness. Analyzing your feelings is a waste of time (though that's what many singles focus on). Analyze instead the fruit of love, your willingness to sacrifice, your commitment to the other person's welfare.

That's what Jesus did with Mary and Martha. According to Ward,

> In our Lord's mind we can see that the *spiritual* welfare of the household at Bethany was the first consideration. The wait of two days was doubtless to enable them to understand more fully their loss, and to draw out more completely their faith. The tie which bound our Lord to them was knit most closely with their souls. If we would be true friends, giving ourselves to those we love, we must put the spiritual before the material in our relationship with them. Marriage or friendship, which is not based on some mutual spiritual outlook and ideal, can never reach perfection.[4]

A God-honoring friendship is one of the best realities of life. A friendship that might also lead to marriage is even more exciting, which is all the more reason we should guard it and make sure it is built on a solid foundation:

> The spirit in which we enter on a friendship, determines its growth. Too often we enter lightly and

without thought into friendship, but if we consider it as a part of spiritual life, we shall be saved from this disaster. In such a case we shall approach it as a serious matter, striving to discipline it rightly from the start, prepared to give our best to it, however costly it may be, keeping it above the material in a spiritual sphere. If we can accomplish this by God's help our life will be enriched by the greatest gift to be found on earth, a friendship such as Christ gave to Lazarus and his sisters.[5]

Now, not only is this how you should treat others, but it is also how you should expect your future husband or wife to treat you. If your potential future spouse is generous with the things that don't really matter—physical displays of affection, cheap words of commitment based mostly on emotional intensity—but stingy with the things that do matter—disciplining his or her love so that it builds you up in the faith and leads you closer to God—then that person is not the right one for you.

Don't sell yourself short. If someone is pressuring you physically, that person is being very selfish and destructive, even though the selfishness and destruction may be masked by passion. You need to be with someone who will honor you enough even to deny you what you ask for if he or she realizes that what you are asking for is not good for you spiritually.

I am so convicted writing this chapter. I *so* did not live this way as a single! If you've messed up, I completely understand. There's time now to do it differently in the future. Put the spiritual first, learn to love in a way that is truly love, and learn to date like Jesus would date. Doing so will help you make a wiser marital choice, and just as importantly, it will help forge the character you will need to have a spiritually intimate marriage.

STUDY QUESTIONS

1. Why is it important when we seek to choose someone to marry that the *process* honor God? Isn't the final result what really counts?

2. Why do you think, given all they had already seen, that Mary and Martha were still inclined to doubt Jesus? What might this teach us about our own responses to God's work in our lives today?

3. Does the way someone dates, expresses their feelings, or makes a commitment reflect in any way on their character, or is that more a matter of personality? If you think it does reflect on their character, how so?

4. How can someone practically apply the words, "To analyze one's feelings is the worst way of arriving at a measure of friendship; to count its cost is the best way"?

19

MERCY MARRIAGES

Never marry for mercy.

If, while reading this, you have serious concerns about proceeding with a relationship, your heart may begin to fight back: "I don't want to hurt him." "It would be so embarrassing to break things off now." "We've told everyone; I can't do that to her." "He's basically a good person, so I'm just going to go ahead with it."

These are understandable and even commendable sentiments, but they are disastrous conclusions. This is where the *why* of marriage is supremely important, and mercy, in this case, is a woefully unwise motivation.

A young woman approached me after I spoke at a church and mentioned dating a guy with a temper who was also somewhat young in his faith. She felt she was kind of "dragging him along," spiritually speaking.

"I care about him," she said, "and want the best for him."

"Good for you," I said, "but that doesn't mean you need to be in a romantic relationship with him or certainly not that you should *marry* him. Let me put it another way, especially since you're so young: is he the *best* you can do? Is this the best man you can give to your future children as a dad? Are you confident that if you wait, you'll not find a man who is less angry and more spiritually mature?"

You have to be realistic. Given what you can bring to the marriage relationship, are you selling yourself—and your future children—short, or is this as good a match as you could hope to make? It's not selfish to want to make a wise marital choice. It is, in fact, foolish to make an unwise marital choice. If you go through with a less-than-wise marital choice, your future kids will suffer for the rest of their lives. You will suffer. Your community and church will suffer the consequences of a dysfunctional marriage. Your spouse will ultimately suffer, as who wants to be married to someone who regretted the marriage even before the wedding took place? Most of us will get just one chance to build a family that seeks first God's kingdom. Wanting the best person to seek that kingdom with is being a good steward of your life. It's being kind to your future children. It's a gift to God's church. It's a powerful witness to the outside world. It's an act of love.

It is absolutely foolish to think the best way to avoid short-term pain—breaking up with someone—is by entering uncertainly into a lifetime relationship. If you know the relationship isn't wise or right, end it. Don't get married. At the very least, delay the wedding. Yes, it may be embarrassing. Yes, there will be tears and hurt feelings. But getting married to avoid short-term pain and embarrassment is like fleeing the country to become an exile for life just to avoid paying a twenty-five-dollar fine for jaywalking. You've lost all sense of proportion.

If you're wavering, ask someone to help you. Go to a parent, a counselor, a friend, or a pastor, and ask for their assistance: "I know I need to end it, but I don't know how. On my own, I won't. Please, don't let me go through with this. Help me to end it in the kindest way possible."

OTHER "MERCY" MARRIAGES

"Marrying for mercy" includes going through with a wedding even after problem areas have been exposed, simply because postponing the wedding to make sure the relationship is solid or to work on issues first means you'd lose deposit money for the hall, the availability of your dream church, or the cost of the wedding dress you've already purchased.

This is short-term thinking, at best. It's like being afraid to shift a million-dollar investment from something risky to something certain because you don't want to spend the time to make a phone call. In the course of your life, where you get married won't matter a millionth as much as who you're married to. The wedding ceremony will last, on average, sixty minutes; your marriage will affect you for sixty years. Don't let something so short term and trivial lead you into something so long lasting and profound.

Another form of "marrying for mercy" is getting married because you had sex and think that now you have to. Letting an act of sin lead you into a lifetime of foolishness doesn't honor God. That's heaping sin upon sin in an attempt to make things right. No, you shouldn't have slept together, but going through with an unwise marital choice won't fix or erase your past sin—only the cross of Christ can do that. Don't condemn your kids to growing up in a less-than-mature home simply because, in a moment of passion, you gave yourself away when you shouldn't have. Marriage is about more than you. It's about your kids, your community, your church, the kingdom of God. Punishing yourself by going through with an unwise marriage because you've sinned is, first, blindness to God's grace and mercy; second, an offense against wisdom; and third, a potential act of cruelty toward your future children.

Listen, it's a lie for a couple to rationalize and say, "If we decide we're going to get married we can start having sex now, and God will consider us married," *and* it's a lie to suggest that one act of sexual intercourse *makes* you married. Otherwise, all those people who are "living in sin" by living together without getting married aren't really living in sin—they're actually married in God's eyes, and the ceremony doesn't matter. Such thinking puts formulaic piety above wisdom and righteousness.

A third form of marrying for mercy is marrying someone because you feel sorry for that person, perhaps even thinking that no one else would marry them. Again, for the sake of the church, your future children, and the potential for you to live the most spiritually influential life possible, this is an act of poor stewardship. It's not your life, your body, your future to give away. We belong to God, first and foremost. We live to please Him before we live to please anyone else. If God calls you to marry someone, you need to be open to that, but make sure it's a genuine call, not an act of guilt or false mercy.

This is *not* to dissuade you from marrying a person who is seriously disabled or dealing with some issues in his or her past that you know will be troublesome. These marriages, entered into wisely by discerning people with hearts in the right place, can supremely glorify God. The motivation, however, must be companionship and biblical love, not feeling sorry for someone. Let a pastor or wise counselor grill you. Make sure your advisor is the kind of person who is strong enough to challenge you or release you before he or she blesses you. If the relationship is right and wise, it will stand up to the strongest scrutiny.

Finally, mercy marriages include getting married because you feel sorry for *you*, so you compromise and agree to marry someone who you know isn't a good match, but it's the best you can find right now and you just want to get the search over with. This is called getting married because you want to be married, rather than getting married because you've found a great match. Desperation and dating are a toxic mix.

Having friends who get engaged over the holidays—particularly if the friends have dated for less time than you have—can make you even more eager to tie the knot. That's why, interestingly enough, a lot of couples break up in January. So many of their friends got engaged that when they didn't, they think there must be something wrong with their relationship.

Resist this pressure to tie the knot just because others are rushing the process! If you make a subpar marital decision, you'll soon *increase* your agony and the pressure you live under, not relieve it. You'll face new pressure, new frustrations, new challenges—and all of them on a higher level.

Getting married to whomever you happen to be dating just because you're tired of being single is like buying a house because it's next to a restaurant and you just happen to be hungry. It might be convenient for that one meal, but do you want to eat there for the rest of your life?

Change for the sake of change rarely works out. Be focused in your pursuit, patient in your search, wise in your final deliberation. We've already said it, but it's worth repeating: any counselor or married person will tell you that single and lonely is easier to fix than married and lonely. Don't take a bad situation and make it *worse*. As my good friend Ben Young says, getting married won't make you happy or an adult; getting married simply makes you … *married*.

FURTHER BAD REASONS TO GO THROUGH WITH A WEDDING

In their book *The One*,[1] Ben Young and Samuel Adams give a few other really bad reasons that people go through with a wedding. Young and Adams don't use the language of "mercy marriages," but their thinking is similar.

"I've invested too much time and energy [in this relationship to let it go]."

This is an all-too-common sentiment, and its danger lies in seriously shortsighted thinking. Agreeing to be married to someone for fifty years because you've been in a frustrating relationship for five years makes no sense. At some point, you have to cut your losses. If you realize you made a foolish decision to get in the relationship, and then made a second foolish decision to stay in the relationship too long, don't make a third catastrophic decision of cementing the relationship.

"I'm scared of what the person might do if [we break up]."

This can go two ways: you might be afraid that the person will hurt you or hurt himself or herself. Either way shows the person's unsuitability as a marriage partner.

If you're scared to break up with someone because of what he or she might do to you, do you want to live in fear for the rest of your life? This is the time to get free, not to maintain the nightmare, and certainly not to create children who will share your nightmare. If you're afraid of angering this person, your children will also be afraid—do you really want to create a family with such a person? I'm not saying you should be rash in this situation. In fact, if you're truly scared, I'm pleading with you to work with a counselor who has experience handling abusive people so that you can learn the safest way to break out of the relationship. But break out of it you must.

If your concern is that the person might do harm to himself or herself, once again, ask yourself if you want to live for the rest of your life with the burden of having to keep someone happy or else watch that person resort to self-violence. This might sound harsh, but you need to hear it: it's never your fault if someone hurts himself or herself because you initiate a breakup, if you do so with integrity and compassion. You shouldn't be a jerk about the way you end the relationship, and you certainly shouldn't be cruel. You can expect the person to show emotion and even anger, but anything else is his or her problem, not yours. If that person's response is all out of whack, something has happened to him or her outside of and prior to your relationship that has led to such a rash response, and you are neither responsible for it nor capable of fixing it.

Of course, you'll want to be extra sensitive. I would recommend working with a counselor, alone, to plot out how to bring the relationship to an end in the kindest, cleanest way. If you do all that you can do to act with integrity, you should bear no guilt if someone else chooses to act inappropriately. Had you stayed with such a person, you would be *feeding* the illness, not curing it. Perhaps your leaving will be the wake-up call that person needs to seek help.

"God's called me to carry this cross."

Really? Has God also called your future children to carry that cross? Has God called someone else to whom you could have been happily married to also carry a cross, since he or she will be denied a lifetime with you?

I remember speaking with a middle-aged woman, divorced, who felt God was calling her into a significant ministry. She was dating a professional man who was economically and socially very successful but particularly young in his faith.

"If you marry this man," I warned her, "he'll become your ministry. You're not going to get much from him, and it's going to take a lot out of you to keep the family healthy. Also keep in mind that you'll be sabotaging this other ministry that you believe God may be calling you to. Are you sure this is God's will for you?"

When you accept a cross, you're limiting your ability to carry other crosses, so make doubly sure you know what you're doing. Because of the account of Hosea, I can't say God has never called anyone into a difficult marriage, but it's clear the Bible doesn't see the case of Hosea as normative.

ROWDY AND ANNA

My friends Byron and Carla Weathersbee have counseled numerous couples considering marriage. One story they tell in their book *Before Forever* might seem sad, but it actually has a happy ending.

Rowdy and Anna met at a Young Life camp and fell deeply in love: "Long conversations while washing dishes led to one of those Hollywood-scripted moments together on the beach. You know the scene. As the sun set, they began to drop their guard in free-flowing conversation and found they had the same vision and passion for Christ. They laughed, they shared, they entered each other's worlds, matching dreams and lifestyle plans. And they both liked what they saw. It was at that moment that Rowdy just knew that this was the one!"[2]

Rowdy transferred to Anna's university so that they could be together and build the relationship, which eventually led Rowdy to pop the question. Even though Anna had told Rowdy (on more than one occasion) that he would need to ask her dad for his blessing before approaching her, Rowdy talked to Anna first. This turned what could have been a very romantic moment into a very frustrating one for Anna and a bewildering one for Rowdy.

They managed to overcome the awkwardness and still got engaged, but the incident itself became a picture of some significant differences in their personalities. Here's how Byron and Carla described it: "Rowdy plowed through life like an ice-breaker through frozen seas.... If Rowdy ever found himself in trouble, he used his charm and humor to wiggle out of it.... Rowdy was a bright, sharp-tongued, make-it-happen kind of guy who lived life in the fast lane."[3]

Anna loved these traits about Rowdy and saw them in a positive light; her parents had a bit of a negative spin. They thought Rowdy could be "controlling, unkind, and sometimes verbally abusive."

Then the Weathersbees uncovered in premarital counseling that Rowdy had some significant debt due to sports gambling (he called it "bad investments"). But, as for most couples, these sobering issues didn't shake either Anna's or Rowdy's confidence. Both thought, *If we could just get married, share life, and regain focus on our vision that we talked about that evening at Young Life camp, then some of those issues would resolve themselves—wouldn't they?*

See, that's what happens. After engagement, couples see issues and think that marriage will resolve them. You've already invested so much in the relationship—you've even gotten engaged!—that the thought of it not working out is too terrible to contemplate. So you just hope that marriage will make everything better.

But it got more troublesome in the case of Rowdy and Anna. When Anna left the Midwest, where she was raised, and moved to New York to be near Rowdy, she was shocked at the reality of city life. She had grown up in the suburbs, "where the greatest dangers included staying out of the path of families out for an evening bike ride together." She soon had her fill of "all that noise, all those dirty, unkempt people, expensive rent for a nasty one-room apartment, and that hectic subway-chasing, taxi-hailing, look-no-one-in-the-eyes lifestyle."[4]

Quite wisely, Rowdy and Anna eventually realized that who Anna was and who Rowdy was didn't mix all that well. While they respected each other, were attracted to each other, and truly cared for each other, getting married wouldn't be the wisest thing to do.

I'm impressed at their character. Think about it: Rowdy had changed universities to build the relationship with Anna. Anna had defended Rowdy to her parents, and then, after college, moved to New York to be near Rowdy. They had spent some prime years together and even announced their engagement to their family and friends. They had invested *so much* that it would have been *so easy* to just go along with the marriage.

But they didn't. They broke up. It was sad. It was embarrassing. It was hurtful.

But here's how the story ends. Today, as Byron and Carla told it in their book,

> Rowdy survives on the money he makes trading futures. Many days he loses big money—but he has also found that he does not need much to survive. He also works full time for a ministry that mentors inner-city kids after school in a rough, drug-saturated neighborhood. He loves the high risk and rewards that inner-city ministry and the stock market bring, as well as the uncertainty and action that each day drops on him. He is fulfilling his passion to serve Christ in a radical way.
>
> Anna is now married to a wonderful man and teaches in a suburban, Midwestern school near where she grew up. Out of the security that her husband and family bring to Anna, she ministers to high school girls who struggle with self-esteem issues and eating disorders.... She is passionate about Midwestern life and her relationship with Christ, and God has brought her a husband who shares similar passions.[5]

It was difficult breaking up, but the ending, as you can see, is very happy. Both Rowdy and Anna have spiritually rich and meaningful lives—just not with each other. They are both seeking first the kingdom of God, but they wisely realized that their respective roles in that kingdom weren't compatible. If you find yourself at an excruciatingly painful crossroads, as Rowdy and Anna did, try to remind yourself of this: *when you close the door on a current bad relationship, you're not jumping off a cliff; you're just opening the door to another life.*

SAYING GOOD-BYE

You may need to seek help if you need to bring your relationship to an end; that's what the church is for. Let others help you carry this burden. In general, consider these principles as you express your concerns:

SOONER IS BETTER THAN LATER

Once you know the relationship has run its course, don't prolong its inevitable end. Don't stay together simply because your girlfriend's sister is getting married in a month and you've already agreed to be at the wedding. I say this because more damage can be done and more hurt can be leveled in a month of uncertainty than in a year of trial and error. It's just human nature. They'll sense you're pulling away, and when they bring it up and you deny it, they'll be able to rightfully accuse you of dishonesty and wasting their time.

I'm not saying you should run as soon as you have any hesitation; be deliberate and thoughtful. If you didn't enter a relationship too hastily, there's no reason to get out of it too hastily. But when you arrive at the point where you know there is no chance the relationship will progress toward marriage, be open, honest, and clear.

BE HELPFUL, BUT NOT A COUNSELOR

When your partner wants to know why you're breaking up, be a true friend and be honest. Compassionately but clearly state the main reasons. Keep in mind, however, that this isn't the time for counseling. If the issue is that the guy has no ambitions, say so: "I just don't see you going anywhere right now vocationally, and that's a huge problem for me." This helps him and chases away some of the uncertainty that creates even more hurt. But then don't get sucked into a counseling session where he might come back with, "Well, what if I send out more applications, or take that internship? Do you think that would be wise?" At that point, be direct: "I'm not the one to discuss this with, and this isn't the time or place, because whatever you do, it's not going to change what's happening here."

Some people, by not giving any reasons, risk creating anger that takes a long time to resolve. You're trying to be nice by remaining silent, but the other person usually takes it the other way, feeling that it's cruel to leave him or her hanging—and that person has a point if the relationship has been a significant one. So if you can find a sensitive, tactful way to explain why you're breaking things off, do so. Giving that person some clues can help him or her grow through the experience, which is kind, but that doesn't mean you become a counselor and try to fix what went or is wrong.

OWN THE DECISION

Don't blame your parents, your friends, or God. You made the call to get into the relationship, and you have to own the decision to break it off.

When you say, "God is leading me to end this" (particularly if the person is less spiritually mature than you are), you're risking making the person angry with God instead of you, when in reality you should be more concerned about how he or she is doing with God than how he or she feels about you.

Your desire not to pursue marriage is legitimate; in the end, that's all someone else needs to know. It's your decision. Own it.

IF IT'S OVER, TELL THEM IT'S OVER

Don't say, "It's time to take a break" if you don't ever intend to get back together again. If the relationship is over for good, say so. It's unkind to leave a boyfriend or girlfriend hanging or to give false hope, just to spare you the pain of watching that person hurt. Hurt will come eventually, because one day he or she will realize you're never going to get back together again—either when you start dating someone else or when more time passes and you don't pursue them. If you give any hope, that person may even expect you to let him or her know if you meet someone else, which will set up another painful conversation.

Do yourself and them a favor: end it completely, thoroughly, and without any ambiguity.

THE HIGHEST STAKES IMAGINABLE

Let me remind you that the stakes are simply too high to compromise on this: *never marry for mercy*. Get married because this is the best person you can find with whom you can build a family that will honor God.

Marrying a person with low character simply because you feel sorry for him or her or don't want to hurt someone's feelings deprives someone else of the opportunity to spend a lifetime with you in a spiritually profitable marriage. You only have one life, one body, one heart to give away. Make it count.

STUDY QUESTIONS

1. What are the benefits, to you and others, of you making a wise marital choice?

2. Have you ever spoken to someone who confessed that they got married even though they knew they shouldn't have? What was their story? Why did they go through with the wedding?

3. Do you believe a couple becoming sexually active should get married just because they are sexually active? Why or why not?

4. What are the dangers of marrying someone in part because you feel sorry for them?

5. Can you think of any other poor reasons that Gary didn't mention of why people go through with weddings?

6. What do you think would have happened if Rowdy and Anna had gone through with the wedding? How can their story encourage other couples?

7. Gary lists the following strategies for ending a relationship. Are there any you disagree with? Any you would add?

   - Sooner is Better than Later
   - Be Helpful, but Not a Counselor
   - Own the Decision
   - If It's Over, Tell Them It's Over

EPILOGUE

A NEW VISION

When Adoniram Judson wrote to Ann Hasseltine's father, asking for Ann's hand in marriage, he didn't sugarcoat the future. Intent on becoming the United States' first foreign missionary, Adoniram was up front about the dangers Mr. Hasseltine's daughter might face:

> I have now to ask whether you can consent to part with your daughter, whether you can consent to her departure to a heathen land, and her subjection to the hardships and suffering of a missionary life. Whether you can consent to her exposure to the dangers of the ocean, to the fatal influence of the southern climate of India, to every kind of want and distress, to degradation, insult, persecution, and perhaps a violent death.[1]

It's not like Ann lacked options. Widely considered "the most beautiful girl in Bradford, Massachusetts," Ann had more than her share of suitors. Yet it was Adoniram who gained her affection, and his letter to her father, sadly, proved prophetic. Once in Burma, the couple lost a child to tropical fever, and when war broke out, Adoniram was arrested for being a "spy." He hung upside down for days on end, suspended from the ceiling, while Ann desperately sought his release. She finally managed to visit her husband eight months after his arrest and handed over a precious bundle: newborn daughter Maria.[2]

Months followed, and though Adoniram was finally released, both Ann and Maria died of fever soon thereafter.

I can't even imagine what inner agony Adoniram went through. He was human—the horrific events pushed him into a nervous breakdown—but he supernaturally persevered and went on to live a life overflowing with faithful spiritual labor.

God may not have called you to the mission field, but I want you to consider what brought Adoniram and Ann together: a mission so large that they willingly faced, and then endured, some of the worst nightmares imaginable.

Let me give you an even worse nightmare, however: a marriage without a mission, a life without purpose, a relationship without any end beyond its own "happiness." Matthew 6:33, seeking first the kingdom of God, will breathe life into any marriage and remains, I am convinced, the single best reason for two people to join their futures together. Such couples aren't lost in simply pursuing a pleasant five or six decades; they are determined to live a life with eternal impact.

Remember the tale of two tears—the two stories with which I began this book? One married person cried tears of frustration; the other was crying tears of joy. I asked, what kind of tears do you want to be shedding ten years from now?

Having been writing and speaking on marriage for a decade and a half, I've seen how much time and effort are spent by people trying to survive and fix extremely difficult marriages. I don't think any marriage is easy. But some marriages really do require an extra amount of maintenance. If you marry an addict or someone who is spiritually immature, for instance, you're setting yourself up for a lifetime of distractions.

Paul says this is one of the main concerns when considering marriage. He points out that married people are distracted, having to spend significant time and mental effort to please their husband or wife. However, some marriages are more distracting than others, while some marriages provide a base of support for more focused service to God.

I ended my book *Sacred Marriage* with the picture of "holy couples." We usually think of saints as individuals, but what if we took marriage seriously enough to talk about saintly couples, marriages where God is unusually present and active, to the extent where one new identity emerges, a family established on seeking first the kingdom of God?

> What if a few Christian couples took this pioneering challenge seriously, and set out to become a "couple-saint"? No longer defining their relationship to God in solitary terms, but working together to present themselves as a holy unit, a pair of cherubim in the middle of whom God's presence is radically awakened?
>
> It is … an interesting invitation. Is there anyone who will take up that invitation for today?[3]

If singles would consider this *before* they get married, if they would purify their motives to pursue marriage, and if they would make this the basis of who they choose to marry, we'd see much more of this. In other words, if you look at the question of why you want to marry before you choose who to marry, you're more likely to make a wiser choice about the who. It's not a choice between either why or who. It's that asking the why question first helps you choose the *best* who.

I ache for the day when people make such wise marital choices that they can pray through where to live to make the most significant impact for Christ instead of praying that they could merely be able to exist in the same house without yelling and fighting. I pray that God will raise up couples who are so in tune with each other that they will be that much stronger to withstand the inevitable spiritual assaults that are unleashed on any productive Christian. I pray Christian believers will conceive and/or adopt a lot of children and let those kids see what a God-centered marriage looks like. I pray that while such couples will certainly need times of support and counsel on their own as they work through the issues of their sin, even more they will be a resource to other couples—of counsel, prayer, encouragement, and example.

You have no idea how much kingdom time is wasted on ill-matched people trying to make their marriages a little less insufferable. I want you to gain a positive picture—a vision for how much kingdom work could be accomplished by two well-matched people working in harmony to seek the kingdom of God, grow in righteousness, and fulfill their unique calling in Christ.

We need more of these families. There can't ever be too many of such families. There is a dearth of these families today. Most of you will get just one chance to create such a family. Please, choose wisely. We need you to make a wise choice.

AUTHOR INFORMATION

Feel free to contact Gary at Gary@GaryThomas.com. Though he cannot respond personally to all correspondence, he welcomes your feedback. Please understand, however, that he is neither qualified nor able to provide counsel via email.

For information about Gary's speaking schedule, visit his website (www.GaryThomas.com). You can follow Gary on Twitter (@garyLthomas) or connect with him on Facebook (links are available on his website). To inquire about inviting Gary to your church, please email his assistant: Laura@GaryThomas.com.

NOTES

CHAPTER 2

1. Debra Lieberman and Elaine Hatfield, "Passionate Love: Cross-Cultural and Evolutionary Perspectives," in *The New Psychology of Love,* ed. Robert Sternberg and Karin Weis (New Haven, CT: Yale University Press, 2006), 280.

CHAPTER 3

1. Helen Fisher, "The Drive to Love," in *The New Psychology of Love,* ed. Robert Sternberg and Karin Weis (New Haven, CT: Yale University Press, 2006), 88.

2. Fisher, "The Drive to Love," 88.

3. Thomas Lewis, "Twenty-First-Century Love: The Neurological Underpinnings of Human Relationships," *San Francisco Medicine* 82, no. 6 (July/August 2009):13, http://issuu.com/sfmedsociety/docs/july-august.

4. Helen Fisher, A. Aron, and L. L. Brown, "Romantic Love: A Mammalian Brain System for Mate Choice," *Philosophical Transactions of the Royal Society* 361 (2006): 2173–186.

5. David M. Buss, "The Evolution of Love," in Sternberg and Weis, *The New Psychology of Love,* 76.

6. Buss, "The Evolution of Love," 76.

7. Buss, 80.

8. Buss, 77–79.

9. Paul Friesen, *Before You Save the Date: 21 Questions to Help You Marry with Confidence* (Bedford, MA: Home Improvement Ministries, 2010), 53.

10. Fisher, "The Drive to Love," 91–92.

CHAPTER 4

1. Kayt Sukel, *Dirty Minds: How Our Brains Influence Love, Sex, and Relationships* (New York: Free Press, 2012), ebook, loc. 3583.

2. Sukel, loc. 3588.

3. *Titanic*, directed by James Cameron (Los Angeles: Twentieth Century Fox, 1997).

CHAPTER 5

1. Plato, *Symposium*, translated by Seth Benardete (Chicago: University of Chicago Press, 1993), 19.

2. Plato, 20.

3. Plato, 20.

CHAPTER 6

1. I'm drawing on the expositional insight here of Dr. Bruce Waltke, *Genesis: A Commentary* (Grand Rapids, MI: Zondervan, 2001), 328.

CHAPTER 8

1. Francis Hsu, *Americans and Chinese* (Honolulu: The University of Hawaii Press,, 1981), 50.

2. Deborah Lieberman and Elaine Hatfield, "Passionate Love," in *The New Psychology of Love,* ed. Robert Sternberg and Karin Weis (New Haven, CT: Yale University Press, 2006), 277.

3. Paul Yelsma and Kuriakose Athappilly, "Marital Satisfaction and Communication Practices: Comparisons among Indian and American Couples," *Journal of Comparative Family Studies* 19.1 (1988): 37–54.

CHAPTER 9

1. Most of these titles are taken from a table in Robert Sternberg, "A Duplex Theory of Love," *The New Psychology of Love,* ed. Robert Sternberg and Karin Weis (New Haven: Yale University Press, 2006), 192. But I've added some and altered the meaning and wording of others for my own purposes.

2. For purposes of privacy, and to keep me from losing all my friends, I've made this a "composite" example based on real scenarios but with personal identities carefully hidden.

3. U2, "I'll Go Crazy If I Don't Go Crazy Tonight," *No Line on the Horizon* © 2009 Mercury.

CHAPTER 10

1. "Making Screen Magic Is in the Family Script," *USA Today,* June 12, 2011, www.usatoday.com/LIFE/usaedition/2011-06-13-Jada-Pinkett-sidebar_ST_U.htm.

2. Dennis Rainey, *Stepping Up: A Call to Courageous Manhood* (Little Rock, AR: FamilyLife Publishing, 2011), 13–14.

3. Rainey, 14.

CHAPTER 13

1. Ben Young and Samuel Adams, *The One: A Realistic Guide to Choosing Your Soul Mate* (Nashville: Thomas Nelson, 2001), 92.

CHAPTER 14

1. Joshua Harris, *Boy Meets Girl* (Colorado Springs: Multnomah, 2005), 102.

CHAPTER 15

1. Paul Friesen, *Before You Save the Date: 21 Questions to Help You Marry with Confidence* (Bedford, MA: Home Improvement Ministries, 2010), 129.

2. Friesen, 123.

3. Joshua Harris, *Boy Meets Girl* (Colorado Springs: Multnomah, 2005), 193.

CHAPTER 17

1. Ally Vesterfelt, email message to the author. Used by permission.

CHAPTER 18

1. R. Somerset Ward, *To Jerusalem* (Harrisburg, PA: Morehouse, 1984), 91.

2. Ward, 91–92.

3. Ward, 92.

4. Ward, 94.

5. Ward, 94.

CHAPTER 19

1. Ben Young and Samuel Adams, *The One* (Nashville: Thomas Nelson, 2001), 150–51.

2. Byron and Carla Weathersbee, *Before Forever: How Do You Know That You Know?* (Waco, TX: Leading Edge, 2008), 27. Used by permission.

3. Weathersbee, 28.

4. Weathersbee, 28–29.

5. Weathersbee, 38–39.

EPILOGUE

1. Cited in Robert J. Morgan, *On This Day: 365 Amazing and Inspiring Stories about Saints, Martyrs and Heroes* (Nashville: Thomas Nelson, 1997), February 15.

2. Morgan, *On This Day*.

3. Gary Thomas, *Sacred Marriage* (Nashville: Thomas Nelson, 2000), 268.